The
Lindsay Lohan
Story

CW01024278

Ally Croft is a national journalist and film critic. She lives with her husband, daughter and enormous DVD collection in north London.

The
Lindsay Lohan
Story

Ally Croft

An Orion paperback

First published in Great Britain in 2012
by Orion Books Ltd,
Orion House, 5 Upper St Martin's Lane,
London WC2H 9EA

An Hachette UK company

1 3 5 7 9 10 8 6 4 2

A CIP catalogue record for this book is available
from the British Library.

ISBN 978-1-4091-3637-8

Printed and bound by CPI Group (UK) Ltd, Croydon, CR0 4YY

The Orion Publishing Group's policy is to use papers that
are natural, renewable and recyclable products and
made from wood grown in sustainable forests. The logging
and manufacturing processes are expected to conform to
the environmental regulations of the country of origin.

www.orionbooks.co.uk

Contents

	List of Illustrations	vii
1	Baby Steps	1
2	The Magic of Disney	10
3	Teenage Dreams	24
4	Under Pressure	41
5	Fully Loaded	62
6	A Little More Personal	90
7	This Too Shall Pass	113
8	I Know Who Killed Me	140
9	Living with the Lohans	166
10	Samantha	187
11	Ups and Downs	208
	Timeline	241
	Filmography	267

List of Illustrations

Lindsay Lohan on the red carpet at the première of *Parent Trap* on 20 July 1998 in Los Angeles, California. (Photo by S. Granitz/WireImage)

Lindsay Lohan and her father Michael Lohan pose at Billboard Live in Miami Beach on 26 June 2002. Lohan's father was arrested on 3 June 2004 for arresting a guest at a party. (Photo by Lenny Furman/Getty Images)

Lindsay Lohan and Scarlett Johansson at the MTV Movie Awards on 5 June 2004 in Culver City, California. (Photo by KMazur/WireImage)

Lindsay Lohan and Wilmer Valderrama at the 5th Annual Latin GRAMMY Awards on 1 September 2004 in Los Angeles, California. (Photo by Gregg DeGuire/WireImage for NARAS)

Lindsay Lohan's father, Michael, on the phone inside Nassau County Court in Mineola on 7 October 2004. The forty-four-year-old was charged with assaulting one brother-in-law and threatening another, and struck a plea deal, including inpatient treatment followed by probation. (Photo by Willie Anderson/NY Daily News archive via Getty Images)

Lindsay Lohan, Fox Portrait Studio at the 2004 Teen Choice Awards on 8 August 2004. (Photo by Ray Mickshaw/Wire-Image)

Lindsay Lohan on the red carpet on 9 May 2005, Cartier Celebrates 25 Years in Beverley Hills in Honor of Project A.L.S. (Photo by John Shearer/WireImage)

Lindsay Lohan performs at 102.7 KIIS-FM's 8th Annual Wango Tango 2005 at Angel Stadium in Anaheim, California on 14 May 2005. (Photo by Kevin Winter/Getty Images)

Lindsay Lohan with Rachel McAdams, Lacey Chabert and Amanda Seyfried, winners for Best On-Screen Team for Mean Girls at the 2005 MTV Movie Awards, 4 June 2005. (Photo by J. Merritt/FilmMagic)

Lindsay Lohan and Jay Leno during Lindsay Lohan, Backstreet Boys and Jeremy Piven Visit *The Tonight Show with Jay Leno* at Tonight Show in Burbank California on 16 June 2005. (Photo by S. Granitz/WireImage)

Lindsay Lohan with her mother Dina at the New York De Beers Store Grand Opening on 22 June 2005. (Photo by Jamie McCarthy/WireImage)

Lindsay Lohan walks with her brother Cody while taking a break on the set of her new music video on 26th Street and 6th Ave. in New York City on 28 September 2005. (Photo by Arnaldo Magnani/Getty Images)

Lindsay Lohan and Harry Morton at the Palazzo del Casino in Venice Lido, Italy on 5 September 2006. (Photo by Jeff Vespa/WireImage)

Ali Lohan, Lindsay Lohan, Cody Lohan and Michael Lohan Jr at Lindsay Lohan's 21st birthday at a private residence in Malibu, California on 2 July 2007. (Photo by Kevin Mazur/WireImage)

Lindsay Lohan shooting a print commercial in McArthur Park in Los Angeles, California on 5 December 2007. (Photo by Todd Williamson/WireImage)

Lindsay Lohan with America Ferrera filming on location for *Ugly Betty* in New York City on 4 September 2008. (Photo by James Devaney/WireImage)

Exteriors of Lindsay Lohan and Samantha Ronson's home as police issue a warrant for her arrest in Hollywood, California on 14 March 2009. (Photo by David Aguilera/ BuzzFoto/FilmMagic)

Lindsay Lohan with Samantha Ronson at the Charlotte Ronson Spring 2009 fashion show during Mercedes-Benz Fashion Week at The Promenade in Bryant Park in New York City on 6 September 2008. (Photo by Stephen Lovekin/Getty Images for IMG)

Karl Lagerfeld and Lindsay Lohan at the Chanel Ready to Wear show as part of the Paris Womenswear Fashion Week Autumn/Winter 2011 at Grand Palais in Paris, France on 9 March 2010. (Photo by Dominique Charriau/WireImage)

Lindsay Lohan and Ali Lohan visit Millions of Milkshakes in Los Angeles, California on 26 April 2010. (Photo by Jean Baptiste Lacroix/WireImage)

Lindsay Lohan attends a probation revocation hearing at the Beverley Hills Courthouse in Los Angeles, California on 6 July 2010. Lindsay Lohan was found in violation of her probation for the August 2007 no-contest plea to drug and alcohol charges stemming from two separate traffic accidents. The words 'Fuck U' can clearly be seen on her fingernail. (Photo by David McNew/Getty Images)

Lindsay Lohan and lawyer Shawn Chapman Holley at a probation revocation hearing at the Beverley Hills Courthouse in Los Angeles, California on 6 July 2010. (Photo by David McNew/Getty Images)

(L–R) Victoria Gotti, actor John Travolta, John Gotti Jr and Linsday Lohan attend the *Gotti: Three Generations* press conference at the Sheraton New York Hotel and Towers in New York City on 12 April 2011. (Photo by D. Dipasupil/ FilmMagic)

The
Lindsay Lohan
Story

Chapter One
Baby Steps

Like Marilyn Monroe, Winona Ryder and Angelina Jolie before her, Lindsay Lohan's name is recognisable even if you have never seen one of her movies. She may be just twenty-five years old, but thanks to tabloid newspapers and gossip magazines, her name is known the world over, her face instantly recognisable. Headlines would make you believe she is just another child star who has gone off the rails, as many have before, from Judy Garland to Tatum O'Neal, and Gary Coleman to Edward Furlong, but there is so much more to know about this talented actress who, while beset with problems in her personal life, has continued to deliver interesting performances as both a child and an adult actor.

This is an actress who, at the age of just eleven, delivered not one but two endearing performances as twin sisters in *The Parent Trap*. This is a girl who held her own alongside skilled comedic actress Jamie Lee Curtis in *Freaky Friday*, aged seventeen, and who delivered a star turn a year later in one of the best teen movies in a decade, *Mean Girls*. She was the youngest-ever host of the *MTV Movie Awards* in 2004, and had even scored a Top Ten hit on the *Billboard* charts that same year with her debut album as a singer. And she was still only eighteen. She's designed a fashion range, and won acclaim for her comedy performance as a guest star in the TV series *Ugly Betty*. Not bad for a girl that the press would have you believe is a disaster waiting to happen.

Of course, Lindsay's troubles – broken relationships, arrests, court appearances – just add to the mystique of this unique young woman. She's shown us her human side in interviews discussing her life so far, and has admitted to stumbles along her road to recovery. A mass of contradictions – she's a movie star who's admitted she didn't set out to be famous; a comedic actress who's just as skilled in drama; a smart woman who wants to be more than just another Hollywood cautionary tale – Lindsay Lohan has the potential to be as iconic as her idol, Marilyn Monroe, and a star who will survive and have a long career ahead of her, too, if she can be strong enough to free herself from her current troubles.

The story of this red-haired, fascinating, headline-grabbing star begins on 2 July 1986, when Lindsay Dee Lohan was born in New York to mother Donata 'Dina' Sullivan and father Michael Lohan. The personalities of her parents perhaps go a long way to explaining the life Lindsay lives today. Mum Dina was born in 1962 in New York, and claims to be a former singer and dancer – she has said in interviews that she was one of the famous Radio City Music Hall Rockette dancers. However, in 2007 the New York Post decided to investigate her claims, and reported that Cablevision, who owns Radio City, has no record of a Dina or Donata Sullivan or Lohan having been employed there. 'It's like claiming to have a degree from Harvard when you don't. It's a big deal to be a Rockette,' a source at the theatre told the Post's Page Six (their famous gossip column). Dina did study ballet and acting while at Sanford H. Calhoun High School in Merrick, New York State, and at the American Academy of Dramatic Arts at New York University, but according to Boulevard magazine, she also learned about Wall Street trading while acting on stage. 'I had friends who were traders, and I was intrigued how the entire business worked,' she told the magazine in 2006. 'While I was working in theatre, I just learned as much as I could about both industries in those years. It was great training for everything I am doing now, and I am in a position to help my children with their careers.'

Michael, meanwhile, had grown up in Rhode Island,

and had been raised in a wealthy household, thanks to his family's multimillion-dollar pasta-making business. By the age of twenty, he had left the family company and was a Wall Street financial trader in his own right. 'I was the youngest trader on the floor of the commodity exchange,' he told Spencer Morgan from the *New York Observer* in a 2007 interview. 'And by the time I was twenty-five I had four seats on the exchange.' A young man with money to burn – he told Morgan he had owned a Ferrari 308 GTSI (like the one Tom Selleck drove in *Magnum PI*) but drove it off a twenty-six-foot cliff in Massachusetts, escaping with concussion – Lohan was quite the catch when he met young Dina in December 1984 in the department store Bloomingdale's, where she worked on a make-up counter. The couple began dating, and were married on 2 November 1985.

Eight months later, Lindsay was born. Her earliest years were spent in the village of Laurel Hollow, on the western shore of Cold Spring Harbor, Long Island. A former whaling village, Cold Spring Harbor has become a pretty resort peppered with tasteful hotels, and is part of a very affluent area outside New York City – Louis Comfort Tiffany, the son of the creator of the world's most famous jewellery store, had an estate in the area, and it is also home to the Cold Spring Harbor Laboratory, a medical research facility that has boasted eight Nobel laureates among its resident scientists over the years. It's a picture-postcard part of North

Eastern coastal America, with a population of less than 5,000, an acclaimed local school and a picturesque main street filled with little museums and shops. Dubbed 'Gatsby Country' by visitors, due to its wealthy residents, beautiful scenery and lavish estates that look like the models for the homes in F. Scott Fitzgerald's classic novel *The Great Gatsby*, it must have been an idyllic place to grow up.

A year after Lindsay was born, Dina gave birth to a son, Michael Douglas Jr. Both children were raised as Catholics - Michael Sr's parents were Irish Catholics originally from Galway, and Dina also had a Christian upbringing - first in a house in Cold Spring Harbor, and then in neighbouring Merrick, where she had grown up.

It wasn't long before Lindsay took her first steps on the road to fame. In 1989, while other toddlers were moulding Play-Doh and playing with dolls, she - at the age of just three - was signed to the prestigious Ford Modeling Agency as a child model, after being spotted by one of their agents. It was an impressive start to her career. Ford Models (as it is now known) has been one of the top modelling agencies in New York since 1946, when it was set up by Eileen and Gerard Ford. Famous models and actresses who have been signed to Ford include Jerry Hall, Courteney Cox, Twiggy, Christie Brinkley, Elle Macpherson, Christy Turlington and Sharon Stone. Based on Fifth Avenue, the agency is highly respected and represents over

2,500 models worldwide. In signing Lindsay, they got their first red-haired child model. 'She was reputedly the first redhead that Ford had ever hired,' Michael Fleeman of *People* magazine told CNN in an interview about Lindsay's career. 'And she was only three years old. So before she could barely even speak entire sentences, she was in show business.'

A contract with Toys R Us soon followed, with Lindsay becoming the face of the toy store in the US, appearing in more than a hundred print advertisements for them. Other modelling jobs included Abercrombie Kids and Calvin Klein Kids, and in-demand Lindsay may have missed out on some of the everyday parts of childhood for work. 'She wouldn't want to go to the birthday parties. She would want to go to the photo shoot,' Dina Lohan told CNN about Lindsay's early career. Meanwhile, Lindsay's uncle, Paul Sullivan, commented in an interview with *Vanity Fair* magazine in 2010: 'Lindsay was doing so much, even at three years old. She did several commercials: Sears, Burger King, Jell-O. Dina was great at going door-to-door to auditions.'

But while Lindsay was busy working as a child model, things were not going so well at home. When she was just three, her parents separated, only to reunite and carry on a tempestuous marriage. 'It got to the point where my father would not come home for a few days,' Lindsay told *Vanity Fair* in early 2006. 'He would come home three days later and be very angry, and we'd be walking on eggshells. It would be a very tense, scary household.'

In 1990, before his daughter turned five, Michael Lohan was investigated for insider-trading. There had been a previous charge of fraud in 1987 that restricted his financial dealings, but Michael had continued to trade and it was decided that he be charged with criminal contempt. The court stated: 'Fraudulently and deceitfully the defendant (Michael Lohan) changed his name to Desiderio and changed his corporation to Donateco, Inc., and set up a commodity futures sales office in Florida employing four to six sales persons who made between 750 and 1,000 or more cold canvas calls, soliciting potential investors to invest a minimum of $3,000 each through Donateco, Inc. Each such solicitation was a fraudulent and deceitful violation of the Court's order.' In other words, Michael had been told not to trade back in 1987, but instead he had set up a company in another name and carried on. He was sentenced to thirty-seven months in prison, followed by a period of five years' probation, and given a $200,000 fine.

He was sent to Nassau County Jail to serve his sentence. The Correctional Center, to give it its official name, is set in the small town of East Meadow in New York State, less than twenty miles from the Lohan home, but Lindsay's mum Dina decided not to let the children visit, or even know their father was in prison. In an August 2004 interview with *Rolling*

Stone magazine, Lindsay revealed what she had been told. 'My mom just said, "Dad's working. He's away. He's busy." I finally figured it out. I was like, "Mom, I'm not an idiot."'

Indeed, it seems a young Lindsay was the one who kept the family together. 'Lindsay was my eldest, so she was my caretaker and she dealt with a lot of really hard situations as a little girl,' Dina told *Harper's Bazaar* in 2007. She also became the family breadwinner, graduating from print advertisements to better-paying TV commercials and appearances, including a comedy sketch on the *David Letterman Show* when she was seven (playing a piece of garbage!) and TV ads for Pizza Hut, Wendy's and, most famously, grape-flavoured Jell-O with comedian Bill Cosby.

The family also moved to Dina's hometown of Merrick while Michael was in prison. It wasn't that far from where they had lived before, but it is a less affluent area. *Vanity Fair* sent journalist Jessica Pilot there in 2010, and she described the town thus: 'No one aspires to live in Merrick. The 5.2 square-mile hamlet is made up of mostly single-family tract homes ... and an array of strip malls colonised by national chains.'

Named after the Meroke Indian tribe who were indigenous to the area, it's a peaceful place where people keep to themselves. 'Merrick is a good neighbourhood to raise a family in,' a local postman told Pilot. Nicole, a childhood friend of Lindsay's, told the *Vanity Fair* reporter: 'Lindsay is not anything but a gifted and humble girl from Merrick. It's a really quiet town to grow up in – it's not like LA, where there's heavy partying and a whole lot to do. Everyone kind of knows everyone, and Lindsay was more embarrassed than conceited about her good fortune [when she started modelling and acting].'

Following on from her modelling successes, the next step naturally seemed to be to win an acting role in a TV series or movie. Lindsay went on a series of auditions and eventually, in 1996, won the part of Alli Fowler in the long-running daytime soap *Another World*. The soap first aired back in 1964 and ran for a remarkable thirty-five years, launching the careers of actors including Ray Liotta, Anne Heche, *Frasier*'s Kelsey Grammer, Morgan Freeman, Brad Pitt and Luke Perry. Set in the fictional town of Bay City, it followed the lives and loves of the Matthews family and their friends and neighbours. It was the first American TV show to feature an abortion, and it became a ratings hit in the 1970s following a love-triangle storyline, a helicopter crash and a few murders along the way. By the time Lindsay joined the series, it was past its peak but still popular with loyal fans, who tuned in every weekday to see what would happen next.

It was a great role for a young actress, and Lindsay played Alli for a year, only being tempted away from the security of a regular TV role when something far more exciting came her way...

Chapter Two
The Magic of Disney

For six months, producers at Disney had been looking for a sweet, talented young actress to play a special role in their upcoming remake of the 1961 family comedy *The Parent Trap*. The part was special not just because it was the lead role – it was notable because it was, in fact, *two* lead roles, as the actress who was hired would be playing identical twins, separated as babies when their parents split (one twin living with their dad, the other with their mum, each unaware the other existed).

In the original movie, British actress Hayley Mills played the dual role of twins who meet at summer camp and discover they are sisters. Mills was fifteen years old when the film was made, and her characters were cheeky teenagers, but when Disney decided to remake the movie in the 1990s, they thought it would be cuter to have pre-teens in the lead roles. Director Nancy Meyers, best known for the hit movies *What Women Want* and *It's Complicated*, knew exactly the kind of young actress she was looking for. 'I'm looking for a little Diane Keaton . . . Diane is so alive on screen, and that's what I want from the actress in these parts.' Her team scoured Boston, Chicago, Minneapolis, Atlanta, Vancouver, Toronto and London looking for the right girl for the role, and also held open-call auditions (when anyone, not just working actors, can turn up and try out) in New York and Los Angeles.

The girl they chose was, of course, a red-haired, freckled eleven-year-old named Lindsay Lohan. 'I saw Lindsay on a tape made in New York, and thought she was just electric,' remembered Nancy Meyers in a behind-the-scenes interview made for the movie's release.

Veteran casting director Ilene Starger remembered the audition to *Vanity Fair*: 'Lindsay was like a diamond in the rough,' she said. 'Incredibly unique, and very winsome. She was charming and original, with an adorable, but real, look. She had red hair, which was somewhat untamed. She had freckles. She had expressive, laughing eyes, a great grin and an authentic Long Island accent. She had maturity beyond her years, but she was a kid, in the best sense.'

When Lindsay got the phone call telling her she

had won the part, 'I started jumping up and down on the bed in my hotel room and I called all my friends. It was so exciting because I never thought that day would come.' In an online interview at the time, she also talked about how she would juggle acting with school. 'I like creative writing because I like to write, and I want to grow up and write and go to college and then do what I have to do with acting.' To keep her school-work up to scratch, a tutor was hired to help Lindsay during the moments she wasn't filming. That didn't mean fun wasn't had on set – Meyers made sure there were games and music in between takes, and Lindsay's entire family, including her brothers and sister, were also there during much of the filming (younger brother Michael had a small role as a boy lost at camp, while sister Ali, brother Dakota and mum Dina had walk-on parts in an airport scene).

At such a young age, Lindsay seemed very grounded about her burgeoning career. Not many pre-teen girls would have been so calm and well adjusted about act-ing in a Hollywood movie alongside acclaimed actors Dennis Quaid and Natasha Richardson, but Lindsay worked hard and delivered two terrific performances as twins Hallie Parker and Annie James. 'I love to act,' she said at the time. 'And when I grow up, I'd like to study acting and have a career like Jodie Foster's.' She loved working with her adult co-stars, too. 'He's so happy,' she said of Dennis Quaid in a behind-the-scenes interview. 'Even if he's had the worst day, he makes everyone happy. He's so much fun.' And, talking about Natasha Richardson, she added, 'She's so sweet and kind.' Sadly, talented dramatic and comedic actress Natasha died in a skiing accident in 2009.

The plot was fun, and a perfect Disney family film. Nick Parker (Quaid) and Elizabeth James (Richardson) meet and marry in a whirlwind romance aboard the *QEII*. Elizabeth gives birth to twins, but the couple divorce soon after, and each agrees to take one of the children, meaning Nick is raising Hallie in Napa Valley, California, where he becomes a successful wine grower, while Elizabeth returns to London with Annie, where she works as a wedding-dress designer.

By chance, a decade later they both send their daughters to the same summer camp, and it is there that Hallie and Annie finally meet. At first they are enemies, pulling pranks on each other, but after one goes wrong the pair are sent to a cabin at the camp together as punishment, and it is while they are there that they figure out they are twin sisters. They also hatch a plan to switch places at the end of the summer, so that Hallie can finally meet her mother and grandmother in London, while Annie will get to spend time with the father she has never known.

Of course, once they make the secret switch, things get complicated. Annie discovers their dad Nick is going to marry gold-digger fiancée Meredith (Elaine Hendrix), so she calls Hallie and tells her to come back to America with their mother to help break up the engagement. By this time, everyone else in the two families, such as Elizabeth's mother and Nick's housekeeper, have figured out who Hallie and Annie really are, even though their own parents remain blissfully unaware, so they all get involved in the girls' scheme to break up Nick's relationship and get him and Elizabeth back together.

Director Nancy Meyers was full of praise for her young leading lady, as she told journalist Amy Dawes. 'Lindsay was a real find. She was absolutely great; she played those two parts with a real clear delineation, not mixing up her characters. I remember at the end of the first preview, [Disney boss] Michael Eisner was standing by the candy counter in the theater and he said to me, "You're so lucky, because in the original we had just one kid. You were so lucky to find these girls."'

She also described the atmosphere on set, in an interview with *Vanity Fair*. 'She was fun,' Meyers said about Lindsay. 'She would come into my trailer, and she and my daughter would play really loud music and dance like crazy.'

Released on 31 July 1998 in the US, the film was a critical and box-office hit, making just under $100 million worldwide. Ruthe Stein of the *San Francisco Chronicle* called the film 'hugely entertaining and more relevant than most family entertainment', while *Time Out* magazine said: 'The light comedy is sweetly timed, the direction smart and assured'. And Lindsay was singled out for praise for her performance as the twins. 'Lindsay

Lohan has command of flawless British and American accents, and also uses slightly flawed ones for when the girls are playing each other,' wrote acclaimed critic Roger Ebert. 'What she has all the time is the same kind of sunny charm Hayley Mills projected, and a sense of mischief that makes us halfway believe in the twins' scheme.'

Entertainment Weekly magazine applauded her, too. 'Responsibility for making this Trap tender rests heaviest on the bird-size shoulders of auburn-haired, freckle-faced Lohan, now eleven, who won the unenviable job of making us forget about Hayley Mills – at least temporarily. The natural, pleasurable 1990s hipness this newcomer brings to her assignment is therefore all the more impressive.'

Meanwhile, Kenneth Turan of the *Los Angeles Times* wrote that '*The Parent Trap* can't be imagined without its eleven-year-old redheaded star, Lindsay Lohan. Her bright spirit and impish smile make for an immensely likeable young person we take to our hearts almost at once. Lohan's the soul of this film as much as Hayley Mills was of the original, and, aided by a gift for accent and considerably improved technology, she is more adept than her predecessor at creating two distinct personalities for the unknowing twin sisters who meet at Camp Walden in Moose Lake, Maine.' Janet Maslin of the *New York Times*, meanwhile, commented: '[Lindsay Lohan] plays the dual role with apparent effortlessness, and with so much forcefulness that she seems to have been taking shrinking violet lessons from Sharon Stone. Trading off English and American accents, and flouncing through about as many costume changes as there were in *Evita*, Ms Lohan easily makes it credible that the two girls could switch places and hornswoggle their credulous parents.'

There was more praise to come for young Lindsay. She was nominated for a Young Artist award at the 20th Annual Youth In Film Awards in the category Best Performance In A Feature Film By A Leading Young Actress. Her fellow nominees included Kirsten Dunst for *Small Soldiers*, Scarlett Johansson for *The Horse Whisperer* and Jennifer Love Hewitt for *Can't Hardly Wait*. Lindsay won the award jointly, along with Jena Malone for *Stepmom* at an award ceremony that took place on 6 March 1999 in Studio City, California.

The Young Artist Foundation is a non-profit organisation founded in 1978 to recognise and award excellence in young performers, and to provide scholarships for young artists who may be physically or financially challenged. Among the winners over the years have been some impressive young actors, including Haley Joel Osment for *The Sixth Sense*, Emma Watson for *Harry Potter and the Philosopher's Stone* and Lucas Black for *Sling Blade*, so it was a prestigious award for Lindsay to receive, especially for her first movie performance.

The powers that be at Disney soon realised what a talent they had found, and decided to offer Lindsay a three-movie contract. While in the golden era of

Hollywood, offering a young star a contract to make more than one movie was commonplace (Judy Garland, Jane Russell and Cary Grant all signed deals tying them to a specific studio), in the 1990s such a deal was unusual, and the fact that the deal was with Disney made it all the more special.

Founded in 1923 by brothers Roy and Walt Disney, The Walt Disney Company (as it is now known) began in their uncle Robert Disney's garage, where Walt worked on making animated shorts to be shown at cinemas. By 1928, Walt and animator Ub Iwerks had created a certain character to be named Mickey Mouse, and their first sound film to feature him, *Steamboat Willie*, was released in November of that year. Just six years later, Walt Disney and his team began production on their first feature-length animated movie, *Snow White and the Seven Dwarfs*. The movie took three years to make, and was released in 1937 to worldwide acclaim (the movie even won a special honorary Academy Award). It was the first of many terrific Disney animated movies that included *Pinocchio*, *Bambi*, *Fantasia* and *Dumbo* in the early 1940s and, following the Second World War, live action family movies such as *Song of the South*.

Disney became known as a company that aimed many of their products at children and families, be it the Disney theme parks (Disneyland in California opened in 1955), the TV shows (such as *The Mickey Mouse Club*) or the animated and live-action movies.

Over the next few decades, the studio would release such classics as *Lady and the Tramp*, *Sleeping Beauty*, *Mary Poppins*, *Pollyanna* (starring Hayley Mills, who had her own contract with the studio) and *The Love Bug*, and while Walt died in 1966 and his brother Roy five years later, the company continued making family-oriented movies such as *Freaky Friday* and *The Rescuers*. *The Parent Trap* was a typically Disney movie for all ages, and the company acknowledged that much of its success was down to its star, and recognised that Lindsay could become the face of their popular family films.

The only problem was that Lindsay's home life didn't necessarily fit the Disney ideal. The Disney name is associated with its family-friendly movies and squeaky-clean theme parks (for many years they wouldn't even allow their male employees at the parks to have beards!), yet their new star's father had completed a prison sentence, and he and Dina had separated more than once during their volatile marriage. Michael did state, in an interview with the *New York Observer* in 2007 that he felt he was a good influence on his children as they were growing up. 'I read the Bible to the kids every day,' he said to reporter Spencer Morgan, 'and we'd pray on the way to school every morning. I had a Lotus, and Michael and Lindsay would cram in the front seat, sit on each other's lap with the seat belt on, and we would pray. And they were only in junior high school.'

Unfortunately, some of Michael's best intentions

backfired. The rules of his probation meant he couldn't leave their home state, but he travelled to California in 1997 while Lindsay was filming *The Parent Trap* after she had been hospitalised following an asthma attack. He was arrested for violating his parole, and sentenced to another year in jail. This was another blow to the family, especially since Michael and Dina had had two more children, Aliana (born on 22 December 1993) and Dakota (also known as Cody, born on 16 June 1996), and his absence meant that Dina was now raising not two, but four young children alone.

'I feel like a second parent in the sense that I helped raise my family,' Lindsay told *Allure* magazine in 2007 about her childhood at that time. 'And I was put between my mother and father a lot. Well, I would put myself between them to try and keep the peace, and I felt good doing that.'

As well as working on her acting career, Lindsay had school to focus on. She attended Calhoun High School in Merrick and Cold Spring Harbor High School up to the eleventh grade, leaving when she was 16. One of *Newsweek* magazine's top 1,200 high schools in the US (it was ranked at number fifty-two), Cold Spring Harbor High is a small school by American standards, with just over 1,000 students, many of whom are high academic achievers. The school prides itself on its curriculum and standards, mentioning on its website that 'typically, 95 per cent of each year's graduating class attends college'.

It was there Lindsay excelled in her subjects, and made friends with her fellow students. 'I made it a point to get along with everyone because if you're an actress, people assume that you think you're better than everyone else. I wanted to make sure that people had no reason to think that about me,' she told Lynda Obst of *Interview* magazine. For the first few years of high school, Lindsay successfully managed to juggle school with her new film career. 'My family – especially my mother – were very stern about the fact that they wanted me in school,' Lindsay told CNN about those years. 'To experience going through high school and have an education. You know, grow up with friends and go through all of that, and you know, have normal experiences. And I've always had that.' Following her appearance in *The Parent Trap*, Lindsay took a break from acting so she could concentrate on her studies. 'It was a gamble for me as a mom,' Dina Lohan told London's *Observer*'s Gill Pringle in 2004, 'because I didn't want her to grow up hating me. But if she'd stayed in Hollywood, she'd be a nightmare by now. Kids need boundaries.'

One of Lindsay's old school friends remembered what life was like for Lindsay at this time. Interviewed by *Vanity Fair*, Jennifer (who did not want to give the magazine her last name), said: 'It was really hard for her to feel normal around us because she was already making a name for herself, while the rest of us were just kids, figuring it all out. She never really got to fuck up, or go through the normal stages of fucking up, that we did. I don't even think she went through an awkward stage. She was always this stage-ready kind of phenomenon, and that intimidated people, or at least, it made me self-aware.'

After almost two years' break, when Lindsay was thirteen, she and Dina then chose a second project for Disney, which would only take her away from school for three weeks, beginning in October 1999. It was a TV movie called *Life-Size*, co-starring model, actress and TV presenter Tyra Banks. Filmed in Vancouver, Canada, the movie is a fun comic fantasy that follows the adventures of young Casey Stuart (Lohan). A tomboy who plays on the school football team, Casey has kept to herself since her mother died, so when she discovers a magic spell book, she decides to resurrect her mum to make everything all right again. Something goes wrong, of course, and instead of bringing her mum back to life, Casey accidentally breathes life into her Barbie-like doll, Eve (Banks). Eve's thrilled to be alive, but Casey realises she has to reverse the spell – the only trouble is, she needs the second volume of the magic book to do so.

When filming finished, Lindsay returned to school, but it was not long before she was offered another role – that of Bette Midler's daughter Rose in a new sitcom called *Bette*. The comedy series featured the famous singer and actress playing a version of herself, a celebrity adored by her fans who lives in a luxurious Los

Angeles home with her husband Roy, a college history professor, and their thirteen-year-old daughter, who is unfazed by her mother's massive celebrity. Kevin Dunn played Roy, and the cast also included such talents as Joanna Gleason as Bette's manager and British actor James Dreyfus as her musical director, while friends of Bette Midler's also appeared playing themselves, including Danny DeVito, Tony Danza, Oprah Winfrey, Tim Curry, Dolly Parton and Olivia Newton-John.

The pilot episode was filmed at the beginning of 2000 in New York, a location that worked perfectly for Lindsay since her school was only an hour away. But as much as she wanted to continue the role, after the pilot was completed the producers decided to relocate to Los Angeles when they filmed the actual series. Not wanting to move across the country, Lindsay sadly pulled out and another actress, Marina Malota, was brought in to replace her. Eighteen episodes were made without Lindsay before the series was cancelled.

Lindsay had lots to keep her busy, however, including school and another TV movie for Disney that began filming in May 2001. The movie was called *Get A Clue*, and Lindsay stars as Lexy Gold, a young Manhattan socialite who prides herself on getting the scoop for her school newspaper's gossip column. All of her investigative powers are needed when her teacher, Mr Walker (Ian Gomez) goes missing, and she decides to find out what has happened to him with the help of her friends Jack, Jen and Gabe.

Filmed in Toronto and New York, the TV movie was the final film in Lindsay's three-movie Disney contract. At just fifteen years old, she had a box-office smash under her belt and was regularly mentioned in articles as one of Hollywood's new crop of fresh-faced stars. Super-stardom was on the horizon, but trouble was also brewing ...

Chapter Three
Teenage Dreams

As many a Hollywood star will tell you, once you make it big in the city of dreams, people line up trying to find a way to bring you back down to earth, and child stars like Lindsay are not excluded because of their age. The paparazzi have no qualms about chasing a famous kid down the street, nor do gossip columns refrain from writing about those first awkward teen romances that the rest of us get to suffer through in private. Zac Efron and Vanessa Hudgens, Justin Timberlake and Britney Spears, Jessica Simpson and Nick Lachey all learned the hard way that, once you're famous, nothing is off limits to the press.

Lindsay learned the same lesson when she was just

sixteen. Having exchanged regular schooling for a private tutor, she and her family began to spend more time in Los Angeles as acting offers came flooding in. It was during this time that Lindsay met young star Aaron Carter and, in January 2002, the pair started dating. The only problem was, he already had a girlfriend – teen star Hilary Duff.

Carter was no stranger to fame himself. The younger brother of Backstreet Boys band member Nick Carter, Aaron and his twin sister Angel were born in Tampa, Florida on 7 December 1987 to Jane and Robert Carter. The couple already had three children (as well as stepdaughter Ginger from Robert's first marriage): Nick (born in 1980), Bobbie Jean (born 1982) and Leslie (born 1986). Like Lindsay, Aaron started on the road to fame at an early age, following in the footsteps of his famous brother. He was performing at the age of six, the lead singer in a local band: 'I was in a rock band that was horrible, called Dead End. The name kind of described us,' he told the US TV station PBS Kids. 'People liked us; we would go and perform at coffee houses and stuff. I was always off-key, and the band was always off-key. They would always mess up – drop their guitars right on stage. I would be head-banging. I had long hair. It was fun, though. I enjoyed it.'

He made his first appearance in front of a large crowd three years later, aged just nine, performing The Jets' pop hit 'Crush On You' before the Backstreet Boys came on stage at a gig in Berlin in 1997. Aaron's first album was released later that year in Europe and in 1998 in the US, and he went on to contribute music to the soundtracks of hit movies such as *Jimmy Neutron: Boy Genius* and *The Princess Diaries*, before releasing a second album in 2000 called *Aaron's Party (Come And Get It)*. Selling more than 1.5 million copies in the US alone, the album made him a star, and he even got his own action figure to tie in with his third album, *Oh Aaron*, in March 2002. Not bad for a fourteen-year-old!

An avid sportsman, from an early age Aaron had played soccer, basketball, baseball and American football, as well as taking part in motocross bike racing ('I race professionally,' he told *Disney* magazine in 2001. 'That's basically what I do with my free time. If I weren't a singer, that's what I'd want to be.') He had also taken up weightlifting by the time he was fourteen, and become a teen pin-up and part-time actor, appearing in an episode of *Sabrina the Teenage Witch*, and also the hit series *Lizzie McGuire*, starring Hilary Duff.

Aaron and Hilary soon became an item, following the filming of the *Lizzie McGuire* Christmas episode. But Aaron later admitted he wasn't the best boyfriend . . . which is where Lindsay came in. 'I started dating Hilary on my thirteenth birthday,' he said when he appeared on the chat show *The Big Idea With Donny Deutsch* in 2005. 'I was dating her for, like, a year and a half and then I just got a little bored, so I went and started getting to know Lindsay, dating Lindsay. Then I didn't want to do that any more, so I got back with Hilary. And then I ended up cheating on Hilary with her best friend. That's nothing to smile about. She wasn't even that good-looking, either. She [Duff] really got her heart broken from me, and I'm sorry for that.'

Aaron's heartbreaking ways created something of a feud – fuelled, of course, by the tabloids – between Lindsay and Hilary, a feud that lasted four years. It was reported that Lindsay left nasty messages on Hilary's answer machine, and was even suspected of egging the Duff family car, according to the *New York Post* in 2003, while the press also reported that Duff had Lindsay banned from the première of her movie *Cheaper By the Dozen* and had written a scathing song about Lindsay called 'Haters', which described her as 'queen of superficiality'.

'This all started because we both dated Aaron Carter, and she went around telling everybody that I was a horrible person who had stolen her boyfriend. She then got pissed off because I worked with Chad Michael Murray after she had worked with him on *Freaky Friday*. She called him up and said all these awful things about me, which she then repeated to the press. I don't think I can take it any more. It's so hurtful. Sometimes I feel like I really hate her, which is pretty extreme for me, because I don't hate anybody,' Hilary was quoted as saying by *People* in 2004.

Certainly, Aaron Carter did nothing to make peace, either. In an interview with *Star* magazine in 2004, he was less than a gentleman. 'Lindsay is a troublemaker!'

he told the magazine. 'She always has been. When I broke up with her in 2002, I said, "Goodbye, I don't want any more of you!" She was really, really possessive. My brother Nick told me to stay away from her.' Aaron may have had an ulterior motive for attacking Lindsay, however, as he confessed in the same interview that he still had feelings for Hilary. 'I'm still madly in love with her,' he said. 'I'm not with her, but that's just how it is. I messed up. I cheated on her, which was very stupid of me and I regret it to this day.'

It was a shame that the feud simmered for so long, because both girls had so much in common and could have been good friends. Texas-born Hilary had begun her career appearing in commercials, opting to be home-schooled by a tutor so she could focus on her acting. Roles in TV movies followed, but her big break came in 2000 when she auditioned for the lead role in the Disney TV comedy series *Lizzie McGuire*. In fact, Hilary and Lindsay had been working for Disney at the same time and had become 'phone pals', as Hilary remembered in a 2005 interview. 'The thing I don't understand [about the feud] is that for a while, we used to talk on the phone way back when I was shooting *Lizzie McGuire* and she was shooting a Disney Channel movie. We were phone pals. Then, all of a sudden, all this bad stuff happened. I was like, "Why would anyone ever do this to me?" I didn't really understand it.

'It's hard being so young and having people lie about you, with millions of people reading or watching,' Duff added. 'It was all about a boyfriend that I had, and it was weird because he caused all this trouble that I didn't really care about, and that she couldn't have cared about. You're kids, what does it matter?'

Lindsay also commented on the stupidity of the feud. She told *YM* magazine at the time: 'It was blown way out of proportion. I don't have anything against her – I don't even know her.' She later spoke about the whole thing in an interview with *Elle* magazine in 2006. 'People just started selling stories. We were two girls coming up, and it was like the Christina and Britney thing. It was easy to write about.'

Luckily, all the reports in the press didn't affect Lindsay's work. In 2002, as the feud was just beginning with Hilary, and Aaron was still in her life, she signed on to the lead role in another Disney remake, this time of the 1976 Jodie Foster-starring comedy, *Freaky Friday*. The original, based on the book by Mary Rodgers, had been a big success, earning three Golden Globe nominations, including one for Foster who was fourteen at the time. It's the story of a bickering mother and daughter who find they are inhabiting each other's bodies for one very crazy day, and Lindsay, with the comic timing she displayed in *The Parent Trap*, was perfect for the role of the daughter, Anna Coleman. And she was teamed with another terrific comic actress, Jamie Lee Curtis, who was to play her mother, Tess.

'I wanted to go to school and be a normal kid for a while,' she told journalist Jeff Otto of IGN FilmForce.

'I went to high school and I did two Disney Channel movies which were fun, just to keep up. And then, *Freaky Friday* came along and it was just like, "Wow, this is a great script, and it would be perfect for me to come back with this."'

Lindsay did watch the original movie before taking on the role. 'This is very different from the original,' she told Otto at the time. 'It's the same structure: the mother-daughter switching places, but my character is punk rock, which is kind of tomboyish, but with more of an edge rather than just being a tomboy [as in the original movie]. I didn't want to try to be like Jodie Foster and do a terrible job and be really embarrassed.'

As well as seeing the original movie, Lindsay made a point of watching some of her co-star Jamie Lee Curtis's movies, too – including the horror movies *Halloween* and *The Fog*. 'I'd seen all her *Halloween* stuff,' she continued. 'They were so scary, but I forced myself to see them with my brother and his friend and I loved them. She's so great. She just has this thing about her when she's on screen that you just can't stop looking. She's really fun and outgoing. She's really cool – a great person.'

Curtis was perhaps the one person who could empathise greatly with Lindsay's life as a young actress. Born in Santa Monica, California in 1958, Jamie had not just one but two famous parents – her father was Tony Curtis, the star of *Some Like It Hot* (co-starring Lindsay's idol, Marilyn Monroe), *Spartacus* and *Sweet*

Smell of Success, while her mother was Janet Leigh, the beautiful platinum blonde from *Touch of Evil* and, of course, the actress who played Marion, the woman murdered in the infamous shower scene in Alfred Hitchcock's *Psycho*.

Jamie's parents divorced when she was four, and her mother remarried (to Robert Brandt, who was with her until her death in 2004), while her father Tony remarried another four times. Throughout, both sides of the family remained in Hollywood, and Jamie attended Beverly Hills High School before studying social work at the University of the Pacific for a term. Acting was definitely in her blood, however, and when she was twenty, Jamie won the role she will always be associated with – that of teenage babysitter Laurie, who is terrorised by a creepy killer in John Carpenter's much-copied horror movie *Halloween*.

She went on to appear in Carpenter's next scary movie, *The Fog* (in which Jamie's mother Janet Leigh had a small role as the town's mayor), followed by slasher movie *Prom Night* in 1980. These three roles (and her return as Laurie in *Halloween II*) earned Jamie the title of 'scream queen', but Jamie surprised everyone when she revealed a true skill for comedy in her next role, as a prostitute in the acclaimed *Trading Places* in 1983. She held her own alongside two comic talents – Eddie Murphy and Dan Aykroyd as the homeless man and rich financier whose lives are unwittingly switched as a bet – and launched a new comic career

for herself which would include acclaimed performances in *A Fish Called Wanda*, *True Lies* and the TV series
Anything But Love. By the time she and Lindsay met on
the set of *Freaky Friday*, Jamie had also returned to her
horror roots to film two more sequels to *Halloween* –
Halloween H20: 20 Years Later and a brief appearance in
Halloween: Resurrection.

As *Freaky Friday* starts, Dr Tess Coleman (Curtis)
and her fifteen-year-old daughter Anna (Lohan) aren't
getting along. They disagree on clothes, music and
even each other's taste in men – Tess is a widow about
to marry her fiancé Ryan (Mark Harmon) whom Anna
doesn't like, while Anna has a crush on Jake (Chad
Michael Murray) and a love of playing rock music her
mother doesn't understand. Matters come to a head at
a family dinner in a Chinese restaurant, when Anna
tells her mother she wants to audition in a band competition the same night as Tess's wedding rehearsal
dinner. They are overheard by an elderly Chinese lady,
who then offers Tess and Anna fortune cookies that
they both open. The next day, Tess wakes up and discovers she's now in her daughter's body, while Anna
awakes and discovers that – *arrgghh* – she is now her
mother. They decide to go back to the restaurant and
sort the body-swap out, but in the meantime Tess (in
Anna's body) has to go to school and Anna (as Tess)
has to go to Tess's job as a psychologist.

In an interview for *Disney*, Lindsay admitted she
wasn't much like Anna in real life. 'Anna is really

different from me because she keeps everything inside. Rather than saying how she feels and confiding in people, she turns to her music. But she has a lot of anger in her because her father passed away and her mother is getting remarried, so it's hard for her to deal with that.'

In the movie, of course, Anna and her mum get to swap roles, so Lindsay was asked how she would be if she was in her mum Dina's shoes for the day. 'I think I am my mom,' she laughed. 'We're so similar; she even looks like me – but with blonder hair. She's really cool. But I don't think I could be her for a day because there are four kids in my family and it'd be too much work for me. My sister is nine, my brother is seven and the other one is fifteen, but the two little ones are just a nightmare. I love them to death and they're the cutest things in the world, but they just don't stop. I think this movie will help teens appreciate what their parents do because I never really took the time to realise how much my mom does in a day, between getting us all to school and running around town.'

A witty morality tale about seeing things from the other person's point of view – Tess rediscovers the traumas of high school, including a bullying teacher, and finds out what a talented guitarist her daughter is, while Anna learns that her mother's boyfriend Ryan isn't that bad at all – the film won rave reviews when it opened in August 2003, and was a box-office success. Lisa Schwarzbaum of *Entertainment Weekly* called *Freaky*

Friday 'a funny, shrewd, no-bull family comedy', and said Lindsay was 'excellent' as teen Anna, while *Variety* said she did 'a fine job'. In fact, in an interview with *Vanity Fair* in 2006, Lindsay even admitted she slightly altered the role of Anna from how it was first written. Originally, Anna was meant to be a goth, but Lindsay wasn't sure that would work. 'No one could relate to the character when she was really goth. There was nothing there.' Before her audition, Lindsay decided to change the producers' minds about how Anna should appear. 'I dressed really preppy,' she told *Vanity Fair*. 'I wore a collared turquoise Abercrombie & Fitch shirt and khaki [trousers], swear to God, with a white headband. And my hair was really straight and pretty and red and blond. My agent called and was like, "What are you doing?!" The studio ended up rewriting the character entirely.'

One thing that wasn't rewritten was an on-screen kiss (her first) with co-star Chad Michael Murray. 'I was *so* nervous, because it's kissing someone I don't know extremely well who's a good-looking, twenty-one-year-old guy, and you have to do it in front of a hundred people on the set,' Lindsay said in a *Disney* interview. 'So I talked to Chad and I was like, "Listen. I'm really nervous. You might not be nervous because you've done it before, but I'm really nervous. Just know that." And it worked out. We shot that scene for two days straight. He's really good-looking, so it wasn't bad, you know what I mean? I know a lot of girls who are obsessed with Chad, so that was a huge plus for me. And he's really sweet too.'

Lindsay also got the chance to sing in the movie ('At the time I was like, "Wow. I can't believe they're going to let me sing. This is really cool!"') and on *Freaky Friday*'s soundtrack, singing the song 'Ultimate' that can be heard at the end of the movie. 'I've always been interested in singing, and I've always been singing and dancing since I was little,' she told IGN Film-Force. 'It's hard right now, because there are a lot of other girls coming out, I don't want to be just one in the pack. I want to separate myself.'

As well as providing one of the songs, she also got her mother a non-speaking part in the film, dancing in the wedding scene. By now, Dina's career was completely entwined with that of her daughter: as well as uncredited appearances in *Freaky Friday* and *The Parent Trap*, Dina was now Lindsay's manager, looking after her daughter's career.

It was a risky job to take. Hollywood is filled with stories – many of them as sad as some are happy – of 'stage mums', mothers who become heavily involved in their celebrity children's careers. Welsh singer Charlotte Church, who found fame at the age of eleven when she sang over the telephone to the UK TV show *This Morning*, followed by an acclaimed performance on a TV talent show, had her mother Maria as her manager until she was sixteen years old. She created headlines around the world when she told her mother she was sacked in 2002. A source, reportedly a member of the Church family, told the *Daily Telegraph* at the time: 'Charlotte's always been strong-willed. She doesn't want her mother controlling her career. She has her own plans, and would prefer it that any career decisions were taken between herself and Sony, and not her mother. Anyone who knows Charlotte and Maria knows they're both strong characters – there's often a clash.'

R&B singer Usher, meanwhile, had his mother Jonnetta Patton as his manager when he began his career in 1992, but sacked her fifteen years later. 'She and I are on great terms, and support each other in our life's endeavours. We are both very happy, but are now working in different areas of the business,' he said in a statement to the Associated Press. 'This is great for me because it means I now get to have my mother strictly as my mother, with no added pressure. At this time in my life, I am simply more interested in building the strength of my family. And in order to do that, I feel it's best to separate my business life from my personal life,' he added. The separation didn't last long (although long enough for Patton not to attend Usher's wedding); by August 2008, Usher had rehired his mum ('He wanted her to come back on board, and she decided to', a source told MTV).

Veteran casting agent Ilene Starger, who worked with Lindsay on *The Parent Trap*, told *Vanity Fair* that, in general terms, she didn't think having a mother as your manager was a good idea. 'It is my personal belief that parents should not professionally manage their children or enter into a business relationship with them,' she told the magazine in 2010. 'I have seen quite a few "stage" parents who push their child into acting at an impossibly young age, when the child really has no idea if it's something he or she wants to pursue.'

Certainly, at the time of *Freaky Friday*, Lindsay seemed happy to have her mother manage her career – after all, Lindsay was only seventeen when the movie was released, not yet quite an adult capable of being in charge of her own financial affairs. In retrospect, however, Some Hollywood insiders think that this close business and personal relationship between mother and daughter may have caused some of the problems that would haunt Lindsay in years to come. *Us Weekly* magazine's Lindsay Powers, who interviewed both Lindsay and her parents during the young actress's rise to fame, was not convinced that her family was the best influence for a young girl on the brink of major celebrity.

'She had a lot of fame, access and notoriety from a very young age,' Powers told CNN. 'She also does not come from the most stable home environment. Lindsay has never really had a stable background to fall back on.'

As well as new movie roles, Dina and Lindsay also focused on a possible singing career for the young actress. 'A lot of the people that I looked up to, the

Ann-Margrets and the Marilyn Monroes, everyone was a triple threat,' Lindsay told *W* magazine about her own ambitions. 'You had to sing, dance and act, and you did it in all your movies.' And she told *Girl's Life* magazine: 'I've been working on my singing for the last two years, doing demos and trying to find my style. I want it to be hip-hop rock, like stuff you'd hear in a club, because that's me every night. Life's too short to stay home. I like to go out. Me and my friends go to dinner, then we go dancing. We always have fun.'

It was clear that Lindsay was growing up. In the summer of 2003, she had begun filming her third major movie, *Confessions of a Teenage Drama Queen* – the first big screen movie she had made that wasn't a remake of another film. Mainly filmed in Canada (although set in New Jersey), the movie was based on the bestselling teen novel of the same name by Dyan Sheldon. Lindsay stars as Mary Elizabeth Cep (who calls herself Lola), a New York teen who desperately wants to be a Broadway actress, so is horrified when she has to move to the suburb of Dellwood in New Jersey and start at a new school. Once there, she befriends Ella (Allison Pill) and cute boy Sam (Eli Marienthal), but falls foul of the most popular girl in school, Carla (*Transformers* star Megan Fox). Lola and Carla are soon at war – Lola winning the lead in the school musical play, Carla getting tickets to Lola's favourite band's sold-out concert – with everything coming to a head when Lola drags Ella into New York in an attempt to sneak into the concert so she can meet lead singer Stu (Adam Garcia).

'Lola is a very vivacious person, she's really fun and really cool, but lives in her own world. But she has a good heart,' Lindsay said in a behind-the-scenes interview for the movie's release. 'This movie is perfect because it shows the reality of how girls act and are with each other. Lola is a good role model, as she shows you that you can do anything you set your mind to, and to not let anything get in your way.'

She even admitted the role appealed because she was a bit of a drama queen herself. 'I look back and I hate how I was in the seventh grade. I was so into pleasing everyone and dressing a certain way. It was just like a huge fashion thing back then, because at my school it was grades seven through twelve, so we were in school with seniors and that was very intimidating. You tend to grow up really fast when you're around older kids, and I definitely went through a drama-queen phase. I'm still going through it!'

It certainly seemed like the cast had fun on set. British director Sara Sugarman laughed about her on-set relationship with her leading lady. 'My relationship with Lindsay was like, "Shut up!" "No, you shut up!" "No, *you* shut up!" We just bantered back and forth, in a very friendly way, just like two teenagers,' she told *Disney* in an interview.

Unfortunately, it was the first of Lindsay's movies not to get rave reviews. *The Village Voice* called it a 'smug, sanitised fantasy', while *Empire* magazine said it was 'a self-absorbed sugar rush of a movie' when it was released in February 2004. Bad reviews didn't matter, however, as when 2004 began, Lindsay's star was on the rise and her plate was full with record deals and movies in the works. Her eighteenth year was going to be a busy one . . .

Chapter Four
Under Pressure

2004 was a year of highs and lows for Lindsay. She would turn eighteen in the summer, but she showed her adult independence at the beginning of the year when she moved into a Sunset Boulevard apartment with another grown-up child actress, Raven-Symoné. Six months older than Lindsay, Raven had also been a star from an early age, appearing as Cliff Huxtable's (Bill Cosby) granddaughter Olivia in the hugely successful sitcom *The Cosby Show*. She stayed on the show until she was seven, and then followed it up playing a younger version of Halle Berry's character in the TV movie adaptation of Alex Haley's (*Roots*) drama *Queen: The Story of an American Family*.

Raven had had a recording contract since the age of five, and continued to act, appearing in the *Doctor Dolittle* movies with Eddie Murphy and starring in the TV series *That's So Raven* for the Disney Channel as she entered her teens. That was her main job when she and Lindsay decided to move in together, having met in 2003 when shooting a special cover for *Vanity Fair* called 'Raining Teens', that also featured Mandy Moore, Hilary Duff, Ashley and Mary-Kate Olsen and Shia LaBeouf.

'We met at the *Vanity Fair* photo shoot, and she mentioned she wanted an apartment and I said I did, too,' Lindsay told *Girl's Life* in early 2004. 'Raven's really cool. She's really honest, and I like that. She's kind of mature, and she's grown up around adults, like me, so we'll mesh well.'

Both girls were rarely home, however. Raven was busy recording a new album and filming *That's So Raven*, while Lindsay was working on a new movie called *Mean Girls*, which was due for release in April 2004. Written by Tina Fey – a writer and performer on legendary sketch show *Saturday Night Live*, and now best known for her performances in *30 Rock* and *Date Night* – *Mean Girls* was a teen comedy about the different cliques of high school, as experienced by new girl Cady (Lohan).

Cady has been home-schooled for years, having grown up in Africa with her zoologist parents. But when they return to the US, she asks to go to a regular school, unaware how difficult it will be to fit in. The most popular girls are called 'Plastics', and initially want nothing to do with her, so Cady befriends two sweet misfits, Damian (Daniel Franzese) and Janis (Lizzy Caplan). When the leader of the Plastics, snooty Regina (Rachel McAdams), 'allows' Cady to join their group, Damian and Janis encourage her so they can learn the group's dark secrets. The trouble is, Cady likes her newfound popularity and forgets her old friends for her new ones, but soon incurs the wrath of Regina when she falls for Aaron, Regina's ex-boyfriend. Soon all the girls are showing just how catty they can be as secrets are revealed and things get really nasty . . . and very funny.

'I would define a "mean girl" as someone who doesn't think about other people's feelings,' Lindsay said in an interview with *Girls' Life*. 'Mean people are really insecure people. You can't change them, or the way they act. They're just mean. They care about themselves, and doing or getting what they want.'

The movie reteamed Lindsay with her *Freaky Friday* director, Mark Waters. 'People will ask me, "Were you aware of mean girls when you were growing up?" But you're just so oblivious, as a boy,' he told the *Seattle Times*. 'Girls are operating on this level of knowing what their status is, and these subtle things like who's sitting where, and guys are like, "Huh?" We're just happy that a girl will talk to us.'

Writer Tina Fey, meanwhile, who also co-starred as

one of Cady's teachers, told IGN FilmForce journalist Jeff Otto that the script was actually based on her own high-school experiences. 'A lot of stuff [about mean girls] came from [*Queen Bees and Wannabes* by Rosalind Wiseman], because there are a lot of different anecdotes and real specific things in the book, but a fair amount of it did come from stuff that I remembered and now it's all sort of blended in my brain. But I did have a health teacher that was kind of like the health teacher in the movie. Like, a really poorly informed health teacher. And I had some of Cady's storyline with Aaron, in terms of her pursuit of him; it was like the fumbling, obsessive pursuit that I was trying to do in high school. It never worked out for me.'

It was clear that Tina enjoyed working with Lindsay on the movie, and that she was exactly who she had envisaged in the role of Cady. 'She's near about perfect, in that I always had this vision of Cady that she had to be this girl that was really beautiful, but kind of didn't know it. And Lindsay's beauty is she's so naturally beautiful that, in that way, she fit it perfectly,' Fey commented. 'And she has a real vulnerability in the movie, but she also seems resilient and strong because, on one hand, you don't want a girl that seemed too fragile, or you'd be worried about her the whole time. And, at the same time, because she's so likeable, she can go all the way to being this kind of horrible *beeyotch*, like, three-quarters of the way through the movie, but you still feel like, "It's this character that I like that's making a mistake right now," as opposed to turning on her.'

A terrific comedy packed with witty dialogue ('Halloween is the one night a year when girls can dress like a total slut, and no other girls can say anything about it'), the movie was packed with up-and-coming stars including Amanda Seyfried, Lacey Chabert, Caplan and McAdams. Many critics praised the movie as one of the best teen films since 1989's *Heathers* (which was, incidentally, written by director Waters' brother Daniel), with Roger Ebert of the *Chicago Sun-Times* calling it 'smart' and Nev Pierce at the BBC saying it was 'perceptive . . . surprising and funny'. In 2009, *Entertainment Weekly* even chose it as one of their best movies of the entire decade, while in 2006 the same magazine gave it the accolade of twelfth best high-school movie of all time, beating *Grease*, *Donnie Darko* and *Carrie*. The movie was also nominated for fourteen Teen Choice Awards and four MTV Movie Awards.

Lindsay was singled out for praise, too. Roger Ebert wrote that: 'She has a quiet self-confidence that prevents her from getting shrill and hyper like so many teenage stars,' while Peter Travers at *Rolling Stone* called her 'perfection'. Journalist Stephanie Zacharek complimented her talent: 'Lohan pulls off the tricky job of playing the straightforward nice girl without ever seeming stiff or bland.'

The movie was a hit – one Lindsay needed after the critical and box-office failure of *Confessions of a Teenage*

Drama Queen – earning over $24 million in its opening weekend in the US, making it the number-one film of the week. It made almost $90 million in the US alone while in cinemas, making it the twenty-fourth highest-grossing movie of 2004 in America, and it also made over $120 million worldwide.

'Right now, she's the reigning teen queen,' Rob Friedman, vice-chairman of Paramount Pictures, told the *Observer*. '*Mean Girls* struck a chord with moviegoers. It's something that not only young girls can identify with, but also older women and men. Lindsay is identifiable. She's not an unreal personality. Audiences can relate to her.'

Lindsay was suddenly more in demand than ever, and as journalist Gill Pringle of the *Observer* noted, she was more grown-up, too. 'When I interviewed Lindsay for the first time on the Toronto set of *Mean Girls*, she gave the impression of being a normal teenager untouched by stardom,' Pringle wrote. 'A month ago [May 2004], the second time we meet, it's in a suite at Beverly Hills' Four Seasons Hotel. On this occasion, she's more polished. And she's wearing, well, a lot less. A sheer, sleeveless blouse covers a teeny black vest. A diamond glimmers from the centre of a slender belly which disappears into loose blue jeans, beneath which peep perfectly manicured toes in strappy sandals.'

Rumours had been circling Hollywood that when Lindsay was out with her friends she was drinking, despite being underage, and there were even rumours of a fling with then twenty-eight-year-old Irish actor Colin Farrell ('I guess we were spotted kissing,' she told *W* after the pair were seen in a club together, 'but it wasn't such a bad rumour to have!') and that Lindsay had had a boob job. 'It's so retarded,' she told Gill Pringle. 'I'm seventeen years old, my mother would never let me. I'd be deathly afraid, and it's unnecessary . . . but I'm glad people think I have a nice chest.'

She later talked to *W* in the spring of 2005 about the boob-job rumours: 'They're totally real. I will admit that when I first started to develop boobs, my friends were like, "Oh my God, what happened, are your boobs real?" Even me, I was in shock because I was so flat that when I got a chest it was like, wow. And compared to the rest of my body they kind of like, popped. And they sit up! I'm young and I only got my boobs, like, a year and a half ago, so of course they're going to look good. I love 'em.'

Lindsay did have a sense of humour about the news reports that began appearing about her, which she displayed when she appeared on comedy show *Saturday Night Live* on 1 May 2004. In an hilarious spoof of the *Harry Potter* movies, she appeared as Hermione, who shocks Harry, Ron, Snape and Hagrid with the curves she has acquired over the school holidays. None of the men can concentrate on 'Hermione's' magic as they are too distracted by her boobs.

Being asked onto *Saturday Night Live* was an honour – the series is an American institution renowned for its guest presenters. The show, which is packed with political and topical sketches, mixed with live music, began back in 1975 and helped launch the careers of Chevy Chase, Dan Aykroyd, Gilda Radner, John Belushi, Eddie Murphy, Adam Sandler and Mike Myers, all of whom have been regular cast members over the years. Even the sketches themselves became famous, with some being spun off into successful movies. *Wayne's World* was based on a regular sketch, while *The Blues Brothers* grew from an idea stars John Belushi and Dan Aykroyd came up with while they were on *SNL*.

And a list of guest stars who have appeared on the show reads like a *Who's Who* of Hollywood – Alec Baldwin, Jodie Foster, Britney Spears, Johnny Cash, Mel Gibson, Drew Barrymore, Matt Damon, Colin Firth, Colin Farrell, Eric Idle, Elton John, Christopher Lee, Bruce Willis, Catherine Zeta Jones, Demi Moore . . . the list goes on and on, with each name more starry than the last. Lindsay was certainly joining an impressive list of names, but hosting *Saturday Night Live* is more than just standing there and introducing sketches. Her job for the night included performing an opening monologue, acting in sketches with the regular cast and introducing the musical act.

She did have *Mean Girls* writer Tina Fey to help her, however, as Fey was still head writer when Lindsay turned up to the iconic Studio 8H at 30 Rockefeller Plaza in Manhattan to perform on the live show. Lindsay's performance on 1 May followed a week of rehearsals and meetings with the writers, as sketches are written and chosen for the show. Following an 8 p.m. dress rehearsal on the Saturday evening, the live show starts at 11.30 p.m., when it is watched throughout the US.

In an interview with IGN FilmForce, Tina Fey recalled a chat with Lindsay that she'd had on the *Mean Girls* set before Lindsay appeared on the show. 'She said, "What have you written for me?" and I'm like, "Nothing. We do it that week." There's nothing to tell. She can't believe that we do it on the Tuesday of the week that she's there. I was trying to think of some sort of *Parent Trap* idea, something where she plays twins. I'm sure my friend James (one of the writers) is going to want to dress her up like Ann-Margret, just for his own fantasy, to film it. I'm going to probably be on hardcore perv patrol that week, with the writers. I'm gonna be walking around going, "Seventeen. This lady is seventeen. Please keep it down. Keep it cool, everybody."'

'It's nerve-racking when you're out there live,' Lindsay told TV interviewer Ryan Seacrest about the experience of doing *SNL*. 'But once you do the dress rehearsal, literally after each skit you have someone next to you pulling you off stage and into your next outfit. It was so much fun; they have so much fun there. It's very weird that I got to host *SNL*!'

Lindsay's performance on 1 May 2004 – technically the eighteenth episode of the twenty-ninth season, in which the musical guest was Usher – went well, and would lead to her being asked back as host twice more, in 2005 and 2006. It also prepared her, in a way, for her next big role. It wasn't a movie, however. Despite still being a month shy of her eighteenth birthday, Lindsay was to be the host of the *MTV Movie Awards* (as the awards show's youngest host ever) on 5 June 2004, at Sony Pictures Studios in Culver City, California.

It was a very big deal to be asked to be the host of the awards show. Broadcast around the world, the *MTV Movie Awards* began in 1992 and has been hosted by stars such as Will Smith, Eddie Murphy, Mike Myers and Sarah Jessica Parker. As well as hosting the show, Lindsay was expected to appear in a filmed spoof of a current movie (in her case it was *Kill Bill Vol. 2*) and, to add to the pressure, she was also nominated herself for the award for Breakthrough Female (for *Freaky Friday*), to be presented by Christina Aguilera and Sharon Stone. She did admit in a backstage interview with *MTV News* that 'I'm nervous, I have butterflies, but it's a great experience. It's a big adrenaline rush.'

Lindsay opened the show in style, dancing with a hip-hop troupe ('They put me with all these dancers who dance every day and are amazing, but it was really fun,' she told interviewer Diane Sawyer) and impressing the audience with her moves. 'I was so terrified! There's nothing you can do [to combat the nerves]. People say to breathe and calm down, but you just have to go for it and have fun,' she said on *Good Morning*

America. She didn't need to worry – not only was her performance as host a hit, she also won the coveted MTV Movie Award for her role in *Freaky Friday*.

It seemed life couldn't get any better for the teenage star, but there was a cloud on the horizon – in the form of her own father. The day before the *MTV Movie Awards*, Michael was making his own headlines. On 4 June, he was charged with the assault of his brother-in-law, Matt Sullivan, at a family party celebrating Lindsay's brother Dakota's First Communion on 23 May, having allegedly thrown a shoe at him. Then, just three weeks later, Michael was arrested again on 29 June and, as CNN reporter Jennifer Styles stated: 'charged with theft of services after allegedly skipping out on a $3,800 bill at a hotel. His unpaid bill included charges for several suites, and room-service orders in one of Long Island's luxurious hotels.'

The report continued: 'Michael had checked out of the hotel without paying the outstanding balance. The management made numerous requests and attempts to collect payment, without success. The incident was reported to law officials and an investigation was initiated by Suffolk County Police.' According to the Associated Press report on 30 June, Lohan's attorney, Marvin Hirsch, claimed that Lohan was going to pay the bill via credit card but for unexplained reasons the charge was not processed.

Michael was released on $250 bail and asked to appear in court on 26 August, and he was later charged with a misdemeanour for theft of services. In an interview with *Rolling Stone*, Lindsay shrugged off the fact that her dad's antics were affecting her own fame. 'My dad's a big boy,' she said. 'He's gonna do what he's gonna do. I don't feel bad for him. And I don't feel bad for me. I can handle it.'

She even went so far as to defend him against the reports about him in the press. 'He's the best dad. He's the most loving, kind person you could ever meet. My parents are working some things out right now. But they've been married twenty years – they'll work it out.'

However, where Michael was concerned, things just went from bad to worse. In October 2004, he pleaded guilty to attacking a New York sanitation worker, and during the summer of that year Dina and Michael finally separated. According to the UK's *Sunday Mirror* reporter Julian Brouwer, it was not an amicable split. 'Dina is now pushing for a divorce,' revealed a friend to Brouwer. 'She kept him around for so long because of the kids, but this is too much [Michael was alleged to have tried to kick Dina's door in].'

'Lindsay is very upset,' another friend told Brouwer. Lindsay lives in California full time, so she doesn't really have to deal with him face to face, but she has changed her phone number, like, ten times to try to get away from him.'

There was much to keep Lindsay busy in LA, at least. As she turned eighteen on 2 July 2004, she went public with a budding relationship she was enjoying with actor Wilmer Valderrama. The couple had been dating since May, but kept their relationship under wraps until her eighteenth birthday, according to *People*. 'We try to keep it more under wraps because it is a lot more meaningful that way,' Valderrama told *People* in an interview. 'At this point, we don't need all the free press.'

While she had denied rumours that they had been seen kissing in May ('He's like an older brother,' she told Ryan Seacrest on TV), Lindsay had actually hinted about the relationship in an interview with *Observer* in early June. 'I'm not dating anyone at the moment,' she told writer Gill Pringle, 'because everyone's taken or too old. The thing that's hard is that when you're looking for a boyfriend, you're not going to find one. Besides, I prefer twenty-four-year-old guys, and that's not legal!'

Coincidentally, Valderrama was twenty-four, which made him six years older than Lindsay. He was also a major star in his own right. Born in Miami, of Colombian and Venezuelan descent, he had won the role of Fez (short for 'foreign exchange student') in the hit US TV sitcom *That 70s Show* in 1998, which also starred Mila Kunis and Ashton Kutcher. As well as appearing in the series for eight years, Valderrama became known as the voice of Handy Manny in the popular preschool Disney TV series of the same name.

However, it was Wilmer's relationships that often made him a headline in American tabloid papers.

Before he dated Lindsay, Valderrama had been dating singer Mandy Moore from 2000 to 2002 and, on shock-jock Howard Stern's radio show, had caused something of a controversial moment when he confessed he had taken her virginity ('Taking Mandy Moore's virginity was good . . . real good'). However, Moore later said to *Elle* that his comments were 'utterly tacky, not even true', and that 'it hurt my feelings because I like him'.

Lindsay wasn't put off by the reports about her new partner (Valderrama later said his comments on Howard Stern's show were misreported) and she seemed very happy in her new relationship with Wilmer, as she told *Rolling Stone*. 'We've become really, really good friends. I love him to death. He's a great guy. He's been there for me, with all this family shit going on. We'll see what happens. If this matures into a serious relationship, he'll be my first real boyfriend. But I don't know – I'm only eighteen. I wanna have fun.'

She also talked about the pressure of dating someone who was also in the public eye. 'It's hard when we go out,' she continued. '[Other girls will] seriously hit on him right in front of me. I'm already insecure, and there are a lot of pretty girls in LA. It makes me feel bad.'

Her insecurity had shown through in other interviews, too. To *Girls' Life* a few months before, Lindsay had commented: 'I'm not as hard on myself as I used to be, but that's what happens when you are growing up - you don't like things about yourself that much. I didn't like my body or my freckles or my red hair. I still don't like my freckles that much - they bug me. My friends have that skin, that flawless, no-freckles skin. Mine is just an annoyance to me. I don't even like to lay out in the sun because I worry I'll get more freckles,' she laughed. 'But then I think, "Suck it up and have fun!" Who wants to sit around thinking about what they don't like about their looks?'

Of course, not every girl was on the cover of magazines the world over. When Lindsay visited the set of TV show *Good Morning America* in June 2004, presenter Diane Sawyer showed Lindsay a pile of teen magazines an assistant on the show had bought that morning. Every single one had Lindsay on the cover, or an article about her inside - the assistant hadn't been able to find any teen magazine she wasn't in.

Another indication of Lindsay's popularity was the 2004 Teen Choice Awards, held on 8 August. She was nominated for six awards - Choice Movie Liar, Choice Movie Chemistry, Choice Movie Hissy Fit, Choice Movie Blush, Choice Movie Actress (for *Mean Girls*) and Choice Breakout Movie Star for her roles in *Mean Girls*, *Confessions of a Teenage Drama Queen* and *Freaky Friday*.

While the awards sound a bit silly (in a good way), the ceremony has become a highlight of the awards season. Broadcast on Fox TV in the US since 1999, the show honours achievements in movies, sports, TV, music and fashion and is voted for by teens aged thirteen to nineteen. Each winner of an award is given their own custom-made surfboard as a trophy.

The 2004 Awards was hosted by Paris Hilton and Nicole Richie, and Femalefirst.co.uk reported that Lindsay 'stole the show'. She picked up four awards for Choice Hissy Fit, Choice Actress, Choice Blush and Choice Breakout Movie Star. Clad in jeans and a pink halter top (this is a casual, daytime ceremony!), Lindsay received the final award from her *Freaky Friday* co-star Chad Michael Murray, and in her acceptance speech thanked her family and 'Wilmer, of course', and her fans 'for supporting me – without you guys I wouldn't be here, thank you so much!'

The summer of 2004 was an increasingly busy time for America's top teen actress. She was due to start shooting her next movie, *Herbie: Fully Loaded* on 4 August, and she was also recording her first album, *Speak*, at the same time. While her career couldn't have been going better, behind the scenes things weren't going so well. All the while, the paparazzi's eyes were on her, and tabloids were filled with stories of her weight loss because she had started to look very thin, her relationship with Wilmer and how she spent her time off in nightclubs (and possibly underage drinking).

'I was living with Wilmer at the time,' Lindsay told *Vanity Fair* in 2006. 'I had to leave the house at four in the morning to go on set. I would literally get home at two in the morning, sleep, then sleep in the car for an hour. I leave the set, so tired from the day, then I'm in the studio until, like, 2.30 in the morning.'

The strain of making a movie and a record at the same time was showing, and it was revealed that, on 21 October, Lindsay had collapsed on the set of *Herbie: Fully Loaded*. At the time, the news was downplayed in the press, but in an interview with *Vanity Fair* in 2006, Lindsay revealed how bad it had been. 'I started to get really bad head pains, to the point where I was shaking in my trailer. I got a fever of 102, and they were like, "You need to go to the hospital." I was like, "No, I'm not going to the hospital." I went back to my boyfriend's house, lay down on the bed. I started getting these shooting head pains. I kid you not, I was lying in that bed and I never heard someone scream so loud. I was screaming, throwing things, because the pains were so intense in my head.'

When she got to hospital, she was quickly diagnosed. 'My liver was swollen, I had a kidney infection and my white blood cells were accelerated. I was on an IV. They were giving me shots of morphine to numb the head pains every two hours. I was really, really white, like a ghost, and my legs were so numb from not walking, I had a walker to walk to the bathroom and back. My body didn't have enough strength to take a shower.'

Vanity Fair asked Lindsay's mother, Dina, about the hospitalisation. 'Lindsay has had bronchial asthma since she was two,' she told the magazine. 'She was shooting in the Valley in 110-degree weather with the full racing suit on, in dust and in dirt. She had an asthma attack. It was the culmination of a lot of things.'

Then came the news that Lindsay and Wilmer Valderrama had split up, on 12 November 2004. The split happened only a few weeks after Lindsay had made a cameo appearance on Wilmer's hit sitcom, *That 70s Show*, as Kim, a girl who comes between his character, Fez and Kelso (Ashton Kutcher). 'Wilmer was my first love, but the timing was bad,' Lindsay told reporters at the time. 'And there were these girls around, he would flirt with them. And I couldn't handle that. I really didn't trust him, so that was hard too. My life was too out of order. I was too depressed. I was too concerned with Wilmer this, Wilmer that.'

Lindsay later told reporters for Female First: 'I lost, like, fifteen pounds. And when I got out of hospital, the whole break-up happened and I lost more weight. I don't really have a comment on it. The thing is, because I was younger, people made it out to be like I was the immature one. I wanted to stay home sometimes and he wanted to go out all the time.'

There wasn't time to dwell on their break-up, however. Despite her hospitalisation, Lindsay continued to film scenes for *Herbie: Fully Loaded* in California and put the finishing touches to her first album. *Speak* was the culmination of a dream for Lindsay that had begun in 2001 when it was announced on her now-defunct website, llrocks.com that she wanted to sing. 'Lindsay is also interested in recording a pop album! It's been said that she sings as well as she does an English accent, so hang on, fans, there may be a recording out by the end of summer 2001!'

That didn't happen, although she did do some demo tracks with Emilio Estefan Jr (husband of singer Gloria), after signing a five-album production deal in September 2002. 'I am extremely excited to be working with Emilio. I am surrounded by a group of very talented people who have made me feel like part of their family,' she told *Business Wire* at the time, while Estefan Jr commented: 'The minute I heard her sing, I knew she was gifted. She is energetic and charming and has a unique style. She is a great performer and has an incredible ability to connect with her audience. I am very excited to be working with her. Everyone will be very pleasantly surprised with this project.'

It was not to be, however. While Lindsay recorded songs for *Freaky Friday* and *Confessions of a Teenage Drama Queen*, an album didn't materialise and her contract with Estefan expired. Then, in July 2004, Lindsay revealed that she had signed to Casablanca Records, with Peter LoFrumento of the label telling the Associated Press that it was 'a long-term recording contract'. An impressive collection of writers and producers were assembled to work with Lindsay, including Kara Dio-Guardi (who has written for Britney Spears and Christina Aguilera and was a judge on *American Idol*), John

Shanks (Take That, Sting), Cory Rooney (Destiny's Child, Jennifer Lopez) and TJ and Taryll Jackson (sons of Tito Jackson of the Jackson Five).

The release of the album was originally scheduled for November, but was delayed until December to give Lindsay time to finish it after her recovery. In an interview with IGN just before it was released, she described what type of album she had wanted to make. 'I love those kinds of club tracks that you can listen to before you go out at night with all your friends. And I also wanted stuff that was a little bit more rock that you could get into if you were, like, angry or depressed or sad. I wanted to be able to touch on all those feelings, and I wanted to speak about all different things, too, which is why I titled the album *Speak*.'

Lindsay wrote some of the tracks herself ('I've been able to write a lot of my own lyrics from past experiences. I mean, that's a big deal for me') while she chose the other songs that featured on the album. 'I was lucky enough to be able to go through everything and say exactly what I did and didn't want, which is hard for a first-time artist to do. You usually don't get those advantages, but Tommy Mottola allowed me to do that and so did everyone at the label, which was very nice.'

The first single to be released was 'Rumors', which *Rolling Stone* described as a 'bass-heavy, angry club anthem'. It was speculated that the song, as well as tracks 'To Know Your Name', 'Anything But Me' and 'First' were biographical. 'Rumors', certainly, was aimed squarely at the paparazzi who had started stalking her. Meanwhile, 'First' was clearly about her (now ended) relationship with Wilmer Valderrama, and 'To Know Your Name' not only talked about her relationship with him, but what it was like to have a romance in the public eye.

It was definitely a personal album for Lindsay, described by IGN as 'an amalgam of slickly crafted rock and dance pop aimed at the youth market, but also strategically packaged in both sound and vision to cater to the older, club-hopping post-high-school/collegiate/über-young-professional crowd'. It was also a hit, debuting on the *Billboard* charts at number four, and staying in the chart for over twenty weeks.

The album's reviews were mixed, but mainly positive. *Entertainment Weekly* described it as a 'grab bag of derivative, low-carb rock songs' and gave it a C grade, but *Rolling Stone* said: 'A surprisingly diverse and accomplished debut, *Speak* proves that Lohan has the mettle and talent necessary to compete with other young pop superstars', and *Teen Ink* said the album was 'a joy to listen to from beginning to end'.

As a tough 2004 drew to a close, it looked like things were getting better for Lindsay, but there were more ups and downs around the corner . . .

Chapter Five
Fully Loaded

It's tough growing up in the spotlight, and Lindsay had done just that. By the time 2005 began, she had already spent fifteen years of her life working, and the last five under the intense scrutiny of tabloid newspapers and the paparazzi. She was also an easy target, as was shown in August 2004 when she had a minor accident in her car and it made front-page news.

'I got into a tiny fender-bender in the middle of the day,' she told *Rolling Stone* at the time. 'The other guy hit me. And the story that came out made it seem like I'd been out partying and got into an accident. I almost didn't get *Herbie* because of that story. They [Disney] thought I was trouble. People in this business build you up and build you up,' she continued, 'then they try to take you down. They'll write what they want. You just have to be yourself – and if people don't like it, fuck 'em.'

Unfortunately, the accident came back to haunt her in early 2005. The Associated Press reported on 3 February that Lindsay was being sued by two people, who both claimed she had injured them in the accident. The report said: 'The personal injury suit was filed in Superior Court on behalf of Eddie Pamilton and Ilex Harris. They claim the actress was driving in Studio City on 3 August 2004 when she struck Pamilton's vehicle, leaving the pair with continuing "pain, discomfort and physical disability". The suit seeks unspecified damages and compensation for medical expenses, lost earnings and income.'

Happily, the suit was found to have no merit, but it didn't stop Lindsay's name appearing in the tabloids. Perhaps forgetting that she was eighteen and had missed landmarks like school proms and teen dating because of her career, gossip columns revelled in reporting that Lindsay was often out partying in the company of other girls such as Paris Hilton, Mischa Barton and Britney Spears.

'I'm the type of person who doesn't really hide anything,' she told *W* reporter Robert Haskell. 'I go to clubs and everything, and if I hang out with Paris Hilton, I don't think that's a bad thing. She's a nice girl. I relieve my stress by going out and having fun. Some people may go and take a yoga class, but people don't care about that. I'll be in LA, and if I drive to the gym, they take that picture but they never use it because it doesn't sell. Because people like the drama. That's kind of what Hollywood's become in a way, as sad as it is, especially for younger girls.'

Not only had the tabloids been accusing Lindsay of having a good time, they also linked her with a host of actors, including Colin Farrell. '"Lindsay's eighteen and she's at a club and she's probably drinking." And, "Oh, she was seen making out with Colin Farrell." I mean, I like older guys. It's easier for me to relate to an older guy,' she told Haskell. 'I have a career, and maturity-wise, to be with a guy that's in college, it's going to be a little difficult.'

The list of famous men Lindsay was allegedly dating was quite impressive – as well as Farrell (who, according to a report at the end of 2004, apparently 'comforted Lindsay about her split with Wilmer Valderrama' and took her clubbing), Lindsay was linked with Bruce Willis, Christian Slater, Jake Gyllenhaal and Jared Leto. Lindsay denied all the rumours. 'People say I meet all these older men and sleep with them,' she continued. 'That's disgusting. God knows where all those guys in the business have been! They should start picking on them a little more.'

The press was determined, however, to prove that she was a wild child. If they weren't writing about her relationships, they were focusing on her nights out.

Haskell asked her about various tabloid reports, including rumours she had taken drugs. 'Scouts' honour,' she replied when asked if she had done cocaine. 'I'm not going to deny the fact that I've tried pot. I hated it. But I've never tried cocaine . . . I've seen how it messes with families, and you know, it fucks your life up. If I hadn't experienced that, I may have gone a different route, I don't know . . . The thing is, people get to the point where they're so bloody desperate that they'll say anything. And you really can't do anything about it because the more you defend yourself, the more it looks like you're guilty.'

Lindsay's problems with her family and her tabloid partying reputation are familiar ones for anyone who has studied Hollywood history. She's not the first child star to have parents who have perhaps been a negative influence, nor was she the first to react to this in a way that would whip the tabloids into a frenzy. One notable actor who had seen this side of fame was Macaulay Culkin.

Six years older than Lindsay, he was born in New York on 26 August 1980. The son of Patricia Brentrup and Kit Culkin, he was the third of their seven children – Macaulay's siblings are Shane, Dakota (who died after being hit by a car in 2008), Quinn, Christian, Kieran and Rory (both Kieran and Rory are actors like their brother, with Kieran having won praise for roles in *The Mighty* and *Igby Goes Down* and Rory for *You Can Count On Me* and *Signs*).

Like Lindsay, Macaulay was working from an early age. He got his first acting role at the age of just four, in a stage production of *Bach Babies*, and followed it with a guest role in TV's *The Equalizer*. It was his role as Miles, alongside comic actor John Candy, in the comedy movie *Uncle Buck* in 1989 that first got him noticed. 'That's when I started missing home,' he told *New York* magazine. 'Being away for three months is like for ever for an eight-year-old, but it was still fun. I mean, my father was pushy and stuff like that, but working with John Candy was cool. He was a fun guy to be around; he was jolly. It's a cliché, but he was.'

It was his next role that made Macaulay Culkin a superstar at the age of nine – as Kevin in 1990 comedy *Home Alone*. It was then that he learned what Lindsay was also learning – that cameras are everywhere. 'It was one of those paranoias like, *There are people in the bushes! There are people in the bushes!* But there really *are* people in the bushes. It was that kind of thing. Hats don't really help,' he told *W*. 'They say if you cover your forehead, you cover eighty per cent of what people associate with you, but it doesn't work. When I was nine years old, I got recognised wearing a ski mask. Maybe it's the lips. I couldn't hide from the world at all.'

Like Lindsay, Macaulay also had the added pressure of one of his parents being his manager – in his case, his father Kit. 'I just remember the exact point when I was growing a little more tired – during *The Good Son*. I had already done one or two things that year, and I just said to Kit, "Listen, I'm really getting tired and I'm not at school as much as I'd like to be; I really need some time off." He said, "Yeah, sure," and the next thing I knew I was on the next set doing the next thing, and it just kind of clicked in my brain: *OK. There's basically nothing I can do to make this stop.*'

Their relationship was as complicated as Lindsay's with her father, and when he was sixteen Culkin decided to take control of his finances once and for all. 'Basically, I had millions and millions of dollars in the bank and my mother couldn't pay the rent because she was spending all of her money on lawyers,' Culkin said. 'We were about to get evicted from our apartment. The only way I could get access to that money was to take my father's name off it, but I didn't want to make it messy, so I figured I'd take both their names off.'

'That's something that's up in the air in my brain,' he continued, 'whether parents should be earning money from their children in that kind of way. That's something for future generations of child actors to figure out, whether parents should be creating that dynamic.'

His life didn't get any easier once Kit was out of the picture. Married at eighteen to Rachel Miner, whom he had met at school aged fourteen, Macaulay made headlines again when they split in 2000, and once more when he was arrested in 2004 for possession of marijuana and controlled drugs Alprazolam and Clonazepam, for which he was briefly jailed – his arrest picture added to a pile of celebrity ones from Mel Gibson to Nick Nolte that have been published the world over.

Was this life of ups and downs and tabloid headlines what Lindsay was also to expect for the rest of her life? Certainly, in the *New York* interview Culkin offered a sad look at the flipside of being a child celebrity. By the time he was twenty, he had no memory of what life was like before he was famous. 'Maybe some spotted memories here and there of going to the park with my mother. But it's hard for me to remember a time when people weren't staring at me for one reason or another.'

That was something Lindsay, and many other child stars, could relate to. Macaulay Culkin's fall from child star to jailed twentysomething wasn't the only cautionary tale in Hollywood. There was, of course, Tatum O'Neal, the daughter of actor Ryan O'Neal, who was the youngest actress to win an Academy Award at the age of just ten for her role in *Paper Moon* alongside her dad. The star of *The Bad News Bears* and *International Velvet* by the time she was fifteen, her career took a back seat when she married John McEnroe and had three children. However, she made headlines at the end of her marriage in 1994 when it was revealed she had a drug problem, and she became another actress with her own mugshot in 2008 when she was arrested for allegedly buying crack cocaine near her New York home (although she eventually pleaded guilty to disorderly conduct, for which she was fined $95).

However, if Hollywood's history may have made Lindsay feel that the only way – with her mother as manager and her father facing jail time – was down, there was one child star whose story may have inspired her, and that was Drew Barrymore.

Born into the Barrymore acting dynasty – she is the granddaughter of acclaimed stage and screen actor John Barrymore and the great-niece of actress Ethel Barrymore – Drew also grew up in the spotlight and had a difficult family life behind the scenes. Born in California in 1975, her father was actor John Drew Barrymore, who is sadly remembered more for his personal life (married four times, he was often arrested for drug abuse and drunkenness and spent much of his life living like a hermit) than for his acting career. Her mother, Ildiko Jaid Mako, meanwhile, was John Drew's fourth wife, and the daughter of Hungarian war refugees. Drew even had Hollywood godparents – Sophia Loren is her godmother and Steven Spielberg her godfather.

Drew followed in the family acting footsteps at just eleven months, when she auditioned for a dog food commercial, and she made her film debut in a small role just three years later in the move *Altered States*. It was her next role, aged just six, that made her famous – Drew played, of course, Elliott's cute little sister Gertie in Steven Spielberg's blockbuster *ET: The Extra Terrestrial*.

Unfortunately, becoming a star at such a young age

had a profound effect on Drew, just as it had on Lindsay. By the age of nine, tabloids reported seeing Drew smoking in nightclubs, and she told *People*: 'I was a club-hopper at ten, as much as a ten-year-old can be. I would sleep over at a friend's house, and we would sneak out.' She was actually taken to nightclubs by her own mother, Jaid. 'My own mum cared about Hollywood and I didn't,' Drew told the *Daily Mail* in 2010. 'I wanted to act and I loved the creativity of it, but I didn't care for the lifestyle. Everyone wants consistency in their family life, and that wasn't the case for me. I grew up in a family that was multifaceted, sexually oriented and pretty much open to everything. And because I was working, my friends were all adults. I had a tough time going to different schools because people knew me from films and I was the fat child who got beaten up every day.'

'I had my first drink at age nine, began smoking at ten and at twelve took up cocaine,' she wrote in her autobiography *Little Girl Lost*. She had been to rehab by the time she was thirteen, attempted suicide at fifteen and then decided to go to court to be legally emancipated from her parents. 'My hedonistic moment wasn't that tumultuous. It just happened at such a young age, so it seemed way crazier than it was,' she told the *Daily Telegraph*. 'Everyone goes to a point when they do stuff excessively, and the majority of people bounce back. Some of them fall into the rabbit-hole – I just got mine out of the way early.'

By the age of sixteen, in the eyes of Hollywood, Barrymore was washed up career-wise. She only got roles in minor movies, had a month-long marriage to bar owner Jeremy Thomas that made headlines, and in 1995 decided to pose for *Playboy* (infamously causing godfather Steven Spielberg to send her a quilt with a note saying 'Cover yourself up'). It seemed she would be just another child star who couldn't make it as an adult actor, but she was determined to get back on track, moving in with musician David Crosby and his wife and working in a coffee shop while going to auditions.

Those auditions led to roles in *Poison Ivy* and *Bad Girls*, and praise for performances in *Boys On the Side* and her brief appearance in the first *Scream* movie. Her hard work and sobriety paid off, and in 1998 she starred alongside Adam Sandler in the romantic comedy *The Wedding Singer* and Hollywood began to take her seriously as a grown-up, skilled comedic actress.

Since then, Drew has had success with movies such as *Charlie's Angels* (which was produced by her own company, Flower Films), *Ever After*, *Never Been Kissed*, *50 First Dates* and *Whip It*, which she directed. It seems the tabloid wild child has finally grown up and learned something along the way. 'I am not someone who is ashamed of my past,' she told Liz Hoggard of London's *Evening Standard* in 2010. 'I'm actually really proud. I know I made a lot of mistakes, but they in turn were my life lessons.'

They were the type of lessons Lindsay Lohan was busy learning, too. She knew if she went out she'd be followed by paparrazi, and anything she did would be dissected in the tabloid press. But even if Lindsay stayed at home with the curtains drawn, it seemed her name was splashed all over the front pages, and once again it was due to her parents' actions rather than her own.

Michael had announced his intention to sue Dina for a portion of Lindsay's earnings – approximately $3 million a year, and in an interview with *W*'s Robert Haskell at the time, Lindsay spoke about her father. 'He didn't do anything for my career, except go out and not come home at night and make my mom and me stay up and wonder where he was and then show up three days later,' she said. 'So I don't think he deserves anything. He doesn't even deserve my respect.' She also talked about his lawsuit. 'I did hear that my dad was suing me for alimony, and I'm like, "I was never married to you!" So what is it for, abandonment?'

More reports appeared in the press about Michael's behaviour. 'Dina is now pushing for a divorce,' an unnamed friend told *Sunday Mirror* reporter Julian Brouwer in New York. 'She kept him around for so long because of the kids, but this is too much. Lindsay is very upset.'

Following his arrest for the assault on his brother-in-law in May 2004, Michael continued to get in trouble with the police. He was arrested in December 2004, accused of beating up a sanitation worker in Manhattan, a charge he pleaded guilty to. However, rather than leave court quietly to attend court-ordered anger-management classes, he made a statement to reporters about his daughter: 'Her friends are parasites and I said so, so they scorn me. They're trying to put a wedge between me and my daughter. We love each other. But the people around her are lowlifes. I have tapes you won't believe, and I'll release them at the proper time.'

He also continued to criticise Dina in the press, telling *New York* in spring 2005: 'All my life, I supported them [his children], I took care of them. All of my life. And then, when Lindsay finally hit, I could see it coming: how Dina was starting to mould, get all her friends around her, have her family around her and start siding with them. It's just a shame, honestly, that my wife is putting my kids through this by not letting them be with their father. That's the part I regret.'

Michael didn't spend all his time pining for his children, as *New York* reported – he had enough time to pitch a TV idea around Hollywood called *The Lowdown*, and to film a pilot for it. The idea was for it to be a show that investigated tabloid stories about celebrities. 'We're going to investigate allegations against famous people and stars,' said private investigator Bo Dietl, Lohan's co-star. 'Each allegation that we have, we're either going to prove it or not prove it.' (The show later fell apart, with Dietl telling *New York*: 'It looks like the fucking show ain't gonna go. I can't be involved with this guy.')

Just days after the *New York* interview, Michael was in trouble again, for following Dina in her car, violating a restraining order and then allegedly parking on the family driveway. 'It's made me closer to my brothers and sister,' Lindsay said about her father's behaviour at the time in an interview with Gill Pringle of the *Daily Telegraph*. 'I've never been concerned about what the papers write about me, but I get upset to read about my dad in the tabloids because I have three siblings and they have to go to school and hear about it. That hurts me most because I feel like a lot of this is my fault.'

It wasn't, of course, her fault. On 28 May 2005, Fox News reported that Michael was sentenced to up to four years in prison following guilty pleas on a variety of crimes. 'Michael Lohan was sentenced to one and one-third to four years for a series of incidents stretching over a year, Nassau County prosecutor Joy Watson said,' read the report. 'The latest occurred in February, when he was charged with drunk driving after running his car into a utility pole on Long Island.'

The charges included the assault on his brother-in-law and, the report continued: 'Lohan also pleaded guilty to aggravated harassment for making a threatening phone call to another brother-in-law, and to criminal contempt for breaking a court order by driving onto his estranged wife's driveway.' Michael was sent to Nassau County Jail, where he would remain until the summer of 2007.

It was from jail that Michael would hear about the latest events in his daughter Lindsay's life. She had finished filming *Herbie: Fully Loaded*, which was due for release in June 2005, and was filming another movie, but her partying – and dramatic weight loss over the previous few months – made headlines in the meantime.

Photos of Lindsay looking very thin and gaunt appeared regularly in the press. In an interview with Gill Pringle of the *Observer*, Lindsay defended her weight loss. 'While I was filming *Herbie* last year, I was working a lot and pushing myself, and then I got sick because I wasn't taking care of myself,' she said. 'I was eating junk food and not working out and not being healthy. So now I work out and I eat healthier and I take care of myself. But still people keep warning me, "Don't get too thin."'

She added: 'I was never on a crash diet because that's not what I do. I could never be one of those girls who throws up after eating. And my mother would kill me if I did anything stupid. But I'm happy to have lost weight, and I'm working at keeping it off. Besides, Kate Moss is my fashion icon. So now I can fit into more clothes and things look better. I lost about twenty pounds, although compared with a lot of actresses my age, I'm actually overweight.'

People were worrying about Lindsay's weight even

if she wasn't, however, and it was a topic that often came up in interviews. When Robert Haskell of *W* asked her about it, following a visit to the doctor Lindsay had that delayed their interview, she replied: 'Even the doctor today, he was like, "Are you anorexic? Are you making yourself throw up? Are drugs involved?" And I was like, "Are you saying this because you've read it in magazines?" Because I don't! People lose weight when they grow up; they lose their baby fat. But, you know, I am around girls, even in the movies, that are like, "I don't feel good, I just ate a lot, I'm going to throw up." Like at the *Vanity Fair* shoot of all the young stars, no one ate. I was going straight to the pasta, and the other girls were eating salad. And I'm the one who people say that about.'

Matters came to a head about her weight when Lindsay was invited back onto *Saturday Night Live* in May 2005. She had made a lot of friends from the cast and crew following her first visit to the show a year before, and many of them noticed the difference in her weight and were concerned for her. In an interview with *Vanity Fair* in 2006, Tina Fey remembered what happened. 'Amy [Poehler, one of the *SNL* cast] was good and tough on her, saying, "You're too skinny," like, "I'm not going to ask you why, but you're too skinny and I don't like it."'

In the same magazine feature, Lindsay recalled that Tina and the show's producer, Lorne Michaels, sat down to talk with her. 'They sat me down, literally before I was going to do the show, and they said, "You need to take care of yourself. We care about you too much, and we've seen too many people do this, and you're talented," and I just started bawling. I knew I had a problem and I couldn't admit it. I saw that *SNL* after I did it. My arms were disgusting – I had no arms.'

In the *Vanity Fair* interview, Lindsay's mother Dina also talked about her daughter's weight loss. 'It happens to people in different periods of their life,' she said. 'She took it a little too far, maybe, and pulled back quickly and is fine. I don't see it as what the press made it out to be. It was definitely more magnified, they took one really bad picture somehow, and they're probably not even her arms in that picture.'

In the *Saturday Night Live* performance on 19 May 2005, Lindsay did look especially thin. With newly bleached-blond hair, she made fun of her figure in a commercial for the upcoming show, saying, 'Hi, I'm Lindsay Lohan, and I am so excited to be hosting the season finale of *SNL*, with musical guests Coldplay, that I haven't eaten a thing in six months!'

During this time, Lindsay was filming a new movie, unofficially named the 'Luck Project', and preparing for the release of *Herbie: Fully Loaded*. Before that, she had the MTV Movie Awards 2005 to attend, where she was nominated for two awards – Best Female Performance for *Mean Girls* and Best On Screen team for her and her co-stars of *Mean Girls* (co-star Rachel

McAdams was also nominated for her role in the movie, in the Best Breakthrough Female and Best Villain categories). While preparing to go to the awards, she made headlines again – this time for being in an accident a few days before – one in which a paparazzo hit her car, damaging it badly (Lindsay was unhurt). In a press conference interview for *Herbie: Fully Loaded* in Los Angeles a few days later, Lindsay talked about the press. 'I have a lot of great things going on right now, and I feel very lucky and blessed for what's been going on, and I've worked really hard to get to this position . . . and I understand these guys are doing their jobs.'

She continued: 'Thank God I had no siblings in the car and there were no children involved, and no one was severely injured. I do have bruises that are very obvious on my legs, but you know, I'm not going to let that get me down. It happens, bruises heal and I'm flattered that they cared that much to want to get my picture. People would do anything to be in a position that I worked really hard to get to, so for me to start complaining about it, it's the price you pay.'

It was the latest in a string of incidents involving the paparazzi chasing high-profile celebrities in Los Angeles (Scarlett Johansson was just one other actor who was in an accident fleeing photographers). It got so bad that less than three months after Lindsay's accident, Governor of California Arnold Schwarzenegger signed a bill that tripled the damages a celebrity could receive if they were injured or assaulted when being photographed. The bill's author was assemblywoman Cindy Montanez, who told Reuters: 'We always said that the only way we would be able to curb dangerous behaviour by these paparazzi was by going after their motivation, and that is being able to make enormous, outrageous profits.'

Meanwhile, Lindsay still had an awards show to attend, bruises or no bruises. *The MTV Movie Awards* for that year were hosted by comedian Jimmy Fallon at the Shrine Auditorium in Los Angeles, on 4 June 2005. Mariah Carey and Eminem were among the live musical acts, while the presenters included Nicole Kidman, Sandra Bullock, Tom Cruise and Hilary Duff.

It was Samuel L. Jackson who presented the award for Best Female Performance. Lindsay was up against Uma Thurman (for *Kill Bill: Vol. 2*), Hilary Swank (*Million Dollar Baby*), Natalie Portman (*Garden State*) and her *Mean Girls* co-star Rachel McAdams (*The Notebook*). In spite of such very stiff competition, Lindsay won the award, and also got to share the success with her *Mean Girls* co-stars when the film won Best On Screen Team and Rachel McAdams won Breakthrough Female, the award Lindsay had won the year before.

Lindsay was thrilled that she got to meet Samuel L. Jackson on stage that night. 'I went up on stage and I started bowing to him, just because I think he's fantastic,' she told an LA press conference a few days later. 'And then when I was walking off stage with him, he was asking how I was because everyone's concerned about the recent accident. He then said, "I've seen *Mean Girls* five times." And I said, "Really? That's really cool. Thank you. It's an honour." And then he said, "It's Mariah Carey's favourite movie, she watches it every night." I've actually heard that, which is so funny. So it's nice to hear that.'

There was no time to rest after the awards show, however, as two weeks later, on 19 June, *Herbie: Fully Loaded* opened at cinemas in the US. It was Lindsay's latest movie for Disney, and the fifth film to feature the VW Volkswagen Beetle car after which the movie was named. Herbie first appeared on cinema screens back in 1968 in the movie *The Love Bug*, one of Disney's most popular family films. In the movie, racing driver Jim Douglas (Dean Jones) gains possession of the white VW car, unaware it has a mind of its own. Jim's mechanic, Tennessee (Buddy Hackett), names the car Herbie, Jim decides to enter the car in a race and the pair end up winning and having lots more adventures besides (including Herbie playing cupid in Jim's romance with Carole, played by Michele Lee).

Hollywood legend has it that a VW Beetle wasn't the natural first choice to play Herbie. Disney lined up a series of cars including a Toyota and an MG in its car park, and invited staff to come and look at the cars – the VW was chosen as it was the one car everyone touched as if to pet it. The decision was a good one, as not only was *The Love Bug* a success, making over $23 million in the US alone (one of the biggest grosses of

1969), but it also spawned a series of movies – 1974's *Herbie Rides Again*, in which he is left in the care of Jim's ageing aunt (Helen Hayes), 1977's *Herbie Goes to Monte Carlo*, in which Herbie falls in love with a Lancia called Giselle, and 1980s *Herbie Goes Bananas*, with more adventures for the car, this time set on a cruise ship and in Mexico. There was even a short-lived TV series in 1982 and a TV movie in 1997, but the new movie, *Herbie: Fully Loaded*, would be the first proper movie to feature the car in twenty-five years.

The movie begins with clips of Herbie's earlier adventures (from the previous movies), that have led him – after losing a few races – to where he is now, sitting neglected in a junkyard. The girl who decides Herbie is the car for her is young Maggie (Lindsay), the daughter of racing driver Ray (Michael Keaton) and sister of Ray Jr (Breckin Meyer), another racing member of the family. Desperate to race again after Maggie's pal Kevin (Justin Long) fixes him up, Herbie tricks Maggie into racing against arrogant NASCAR champ Trip Murphy (Matt Dillon), a race Herbie wins.

Murphy wants a rematch, even though he doesn't know who he was racing (Maggie had a racing suit and helmet on and he never saw her face), but Herbie is upset when Maggie agrees to race for 'pink slips' – meaning the winner gets the loser's car – so he loses intentionally and is towed away by Trip's mechanic. Maggie decides to get Herbie back so she can race professionally, but discovers Trip has sold him to a demolition derby where poor Herbie could be crushed. The pair are reunited, of course, and Herbie and Maggie decide to race in a stock-car race that her brother can't drive in due to an injury. Without her father knowing, she enters the race and is doing well, but Trip is on hand, possibly to spoil everything in a tense finale.

The movie, which harked back to the classic Disney family films of the 1950s and 1960s, was a hit, making over $140 million worldwide. The reviews, meanwhile, were mixed, with some saying that while children would love the movie, adults would be bored, but Lindsay was often singled out for praise. Neil Smith of the BBC noted her 'feisty charm', while the *New York Times* said she was 'a genuine star who combines a tomboyish spunk with a sexy, head-turning strut, executed with minimal self-consciousness. Likeable but never saccharine, confident but not snooty, and endowed with the natural freckle-faced beauty of an eighteen-year-old Everywoman, Lohan seems completely at home on the screen.'

Lindsay, despite becoming ill during filming, had immersed herself in the role, beginning when she was driven by racing experts around a track at speeds of 160mph so she could get a feel for what it was like to drive a racing car. 'When I first got in, I was quite frightened,' she confessed at an LA press conference for the film. 'I was sitting there and gripping onto the

Above: Lindsay Lohan at the premiere of *Parent Trap*.
(Photo by S. Granitz/WireImage)

Above right: Lindsay Lohan with her father Michael Lohan.
(Photo by Lenny Furman/Getty Images)

Right: Lindsay Lohan and Scarlett Johansson.
(Photo by KMazur/WireImage)

Right: Lindsay Lohan.
(Photo by Ray Mickshaw/WireImage)

Above: Lindsay Lohan and
Wilmer Valderrama.
(Photo by Gregg DeGuire/WireImage
for NARAS)

Left: Michael Lohan.
(Photo by Willie Anderson/NY Daily
News archive via Getty Images)

Lindsay Lohan on the red carpet.

(Photo by John Shearer/WireImage)

Right: Lindsay Lohan performs at 102.7 KIIS-FM's 8th Annual Wango Tango.

(Photo by Kevin Winter/Getty Images)

Below: Lindsay Lohan with *Mean Girls* co-stars Rachel McAdams, Lacey Chabert and Amanda Seyfried at the 2005 MTV Movie Awards.

(Photo by J. Merritt/FilmMagic)

Lindsay Lohan on *The Tonight Show with Jay Leno*.

Over page: Lindsay Lohan with her mother Dina.

sides of the seat. But then it gets so hot you feel it through the gloves. It was really scary because you get very close to the wall. So you feel like you're actually going to crash into it, and there's nothing you can do. But after that feeling, you're like, "I'm glad I did that, it was a great experience!" It was very exhilarating, so it was fun.'

Like many people who have seen the *Herbie* movies, Lindsay fell in love with the little white VW Beetle. 'Whenever someone gets their own car, it becomes their baby. In the movie, you form a bond with this car and you feel for it,' she told the press-conference journalists. 'He's the underdog, and everyone always roots for the underdog, which is nice to see on film. My character forms a really great relationship with the car as well.'

It wasn't the easiest role to play, as Lindsay had to talk to the car as if it understood her. 'At first I thought it was silly. It's like, "How am I going to talk to a car?" But I wanted to bring the relationship to life and have people really see how cute Herbie could be . . . it's kind of like a pet in a way,' she said.

At the press conference, Lindsay also laughed about a rumour that had been buzzing around Hollywood – that Disney, worried that her revealing cleavage in the movie was too adult for family audiences, had digitally reduced her boobs in every scene. 'Oh, goodness gracious . . . what do you think? To go through every scene . . . do you know how much money that would cost, first of all? And second, that would take so much time . . . that is so silly,' she laughed. 'People have a lot of time on their hands, it seems. I don't know what I did to deserve people saying those things about me. My sister was the one who told me that, and she's eleven. That was the one reason why it made me angry. But no, that's not true. It's flattering!'

Following her Los Angeles press conference and the movie's première, it was time for Lindsay to travel the world to promote the movie. By late July she had arrived in London as part of a European press tour, but her personal life was putting her under increasing strain. With her father in jail and her mother starting divorce proceedings, on 28 July the *Daily Mail* in London reported that Lindsay was leaving the press tour and heading home. 'Lindsay Lohan is missing her own premiere in London tonight to fly back to her mother for the start of her parents' divorce proceedings,' commented the report. A spokeswoman for Lindsay added: 'Lindsay has decided to leave the *Herbie* tour to join her mother and siblings in New York for the start of her parents' divorce trial.'

A year later, Lindsay told *Vanity Fair* that there had been more going on behind the scenes. 'I started writing the song ['Confessions Of A Broken Heart', a song about her father] and I literally had a breakdown in the hotel room, went to my publicist's hotel room and sat there and just cried, and started calling the Nassau County jail. Next thing you know, I'm on the phone with a guard. I'm like, "My father's in there – you need to put me on the phone with him!" I said, "This is not right. I'm Lindsay Lohan, Michael Lohan's daughter.'" According to the *Vanity Fair* article, Lindsay didn't get to speak to her father, so she called her brother Michael back home instead. 'I told him, "I'm coming home, I'm quitting this press tour. I need to get home. I don't care if I never work again. I need to be with my family."'

Her parents' divorce ended up being a long, drawn-out affair that would not be resolved for another two years, but while her personal life was tumultuous, Lindsay's professional life was still going well. She had a new movie in the works, *Just My Luck*, which was due for release in 2006, and she had also been offered a role in acclaimed director Robert Altman's (*The Player*, *Gosford Park*) new film, *A Prairie Home Companion*, alongside Meryl Streep. And if that wasn't impressive enough, Lindsay had another accolade coming her way – she was to have a doll made in her likeness by Mattel, the toy company that makes Barbie dolls.

The doll was to be part of Mattel's My Scene range, which was created in 2002. As Anne D'Innocenzio of the Associated Press reported, the range of dolls was devised as a hip alternative to traditional Barbie dolls: 'Forget pink ballgowns and feather boas,' she wrote. 'This Barbie's got attitude. A new kind of Barbie doll has hit the stores, one with platform shoes, low-rise jeans, heavier make-up and an exposed navel. Called

My Scene Barbie, the doll is Mattel's attempt to stop girls from growing out of Barbie too fast, too soon – and from defecting to Bratz, a line of funky dolls with sultry eyes and oversized heads that have become must-haves for the eight-to-twelve age group since their launch more than a year ago.'

Originally, three My Scene dolls were made: a My Scene Barbie as well as dolls called Chelsea and Madison. Then others were added, including Nolee and male dolls Bryant and Hudson, and later Delancey, Ellis and Kenzie. Often, the release of new dolls was accompanied by a DVD featuring video clips, music and games, but in 2004 Mattel decided to make My Scene movies, beginning with short films *Jammin' in Jamaica* and then *Masquerade Madness*. The third movie was to be something special – a full-length feature starring a well-known voice: Lindsay Lohan, playing herself. And because her animated character appeared in the movie, Mattel decided to make an accompanying doll in Lindsay's likeness.

The story of the animated movie – *My Scene Goes Hollywood* – was simple. The My Scene girls are at school in New York and discover a new action movie is being filmed there, starring Lindsay Lohan and (fictional) Ryan Ridley. The girls (Barbie, Delancey, Chelsea, Madison and Nolee) decide to go and watch, and then get the idea to sneak on the film as extras, believing they will end up as Lindsay's new best friends.

Instead, they learn that being on set is hard work.

Madison ends up getting a bigger role in the film and starts acting like a diva and the friends fall out, but Lindsay gets them all to make up before the red-carpet première at the end. *Aww* . . . The film was released on DVD in August 2005, with Lindsay's own My Scene doll on sale two months later. While it didn't look much like her (though it did have red hair!), the doll sold well, and was a hit among little girls who liked that the doll came with its own pink director's chair, bucket of popcorn, trendy accessories and Hollywood star!

Lindsay herself was now a huge star with her own doll, but that just made the paparazzi even more interested in her. Wherever she went, day or night, she knew there would be cameramen following her, and once again, on 4 October, she had an accident in her car while being chased. MTV reported at the time that: 'Lindsay Lohan was transported to a hospital for minor injuries after she crashed her car into another vehicle in West Hollywood.'

The report went on: 'The nineteen-year-old-actress was driving north on Robertson Boulevard just before 5 p.m. when she collided into the passenger side of a Chevrolet Astro van, according to the Los Angeles County Sheriff's Department. The van, which was turning in front of her, then collided with a parked van. A passenger in Lohan's car and the driver of the Astro suffered moderate injuries.'

A witness told the Associated Press that Lindsay ran from the car into the Hideaway House Antiques store, presumably to hide from photographers. In her 2006 *Vanity Fair* interview, Lindsay spoke about the accident. 'My first instinct was: "Get out of this car, they're going to start taking pictures." I ran into this antiques store that's called Hideaway House Antiques – I mean, the irony of that is just creepy and weird. [The paparazzi] ran down, and I saw them out the window, and I ran into the corner and sat down on this old chair, and I look down and there's blood specks all over the chair! I looked at my assistant. I said, "Buy this chair. It's not getting sold on eBay!"'

According to the Associated Press, as reported by MTV, witnesses said they had seen dozens of paparazzi following Lindsay's car before the crash. One said they had tried to take pictures of her in a clothes shop and then followed her to her car. 'She got into her black Mercedes across the street, and they literally were like sitting on her car, trying to take pictures of her. She was yelling at them to get off,' Lori Satzberg told the Associated Press.

The accident would come back to haunt her two years later when the driver of the van, Raymundo Ortega, filed a negligence lawsuit against Lindsay, claiming she had been drinking before she crashed into his van. In October 2007, she counter-sued, claiming Ortega was 'negligent in the ownership, operation, repairs and maintenance' of his vehicle.

She also said he made an illegal U-turn in front of her, causing the crash. The case went on to the end of 2007, with Ortega seeking $200,000 in damages, and he also sued The Ivy restaurant, where he claimed she was served drinks prior to the accident. That part of the lawsuit was later dropped by Ortega, and it was reported that he and Lindsay settled their case on 23 February 2008.

It seemed that everyone wanted a piece of Lindsay, and there was even more trauma to come . . .

Chapter Six
A Little More Personal

2005 had been a year of ups and downs for Lindsay. She'd had hit movies, awards and even a doll made in her likeness, but she had also endured endless press attention, her father's imprisonment and a series of car crashes that made headlines even when they were minor incidents.

Before the year was over, Lindsay did have something to celebrate, though – the release of her second album, *A Little More Personal (Raw)*. And personal it was – she co-wrote seven of the songs featured on the disc. Before the album's release in December 2005, one of the songs closest to Lindsay's heart was released as a single: 'Confessions Of A Broken Heart (Daughter To

Father)'. Released on 8 November 2005, the song was co-written by Kara DioGuardi and was clearly meant for Lindsay's own father, Michael. The lyrics were particularly sad, and appeared to strongly show Lindsay's wish for a supportive, loving father. The song had been written just before Lindsay quit the European press tour for *Herbie: Fully Loaded*, and it was so personal that Casablanca Records chairman Tommy Mottola decided she would be the best person to direct the accompanying video, as he told MTV's Jennifer Vineyard at the time. 'I told her, "No one can direct this video better than you," he said. "No one knows this song better than you, no one knows this situation better than you." It's a lot to take on, but I told her she's ready, and we'll give her all the support she needs.'

Both Vineyard from MTV and Evgenia Peretz of *Vanity Fair* were invited along to see Lindsay make her directorial debut. The video tells a story, all played out in rooms that are actually shop fronts so passers-by can witness it all. A father (actor Drake Andrew, resembling Lindsay's father Michael) comes home to find a mother (Victoria Hay, as Dina) reading a magazine while his most recent arrest for drink-driving is on the TV news. Furious, the dad knocks his wife to the floor and drags her by her hair across the room. The fight catches the eye of passers-by, who all stop to look, as do the police. Meanwhile, Lindsay is in the bathroom, and her sister Aliana (eleven years old at the time, and playing herself) is in her bedroom, both of them hearing everything. Lindsay throws things around the bathroom while she sings, her sister cries and calls for help.

'This is set in a storefront, on display, because my life is on display,' Lindsay told Vineyard during the shoot. 'This is all real, by the way. It happened.'

'It's a therapy,' she says of the video to Peretz. 'It's like, the best acting that I've ever been able to do is in this video. I freak out and just kind of go with it and create my own scene. It's offensive, and I want it to be. I'm saying, Dad's what I needed: I was seeking your comfort and I didn't have it.'

Dina Lohan, Lindsay's mother, was also on set, and commented to MTV about allowing both her daughters to appear in the video. 'This was their decision. Lindsay wanted to do this, Ali wanted to be in it. I'm just hoping this helps her vent, like therapy. She didn't bring it on. Her dad did. This is her story, and how am I going to stop that? I wouldn't, I wouldn't try to.'

Lindsay knew what she wanted to appear in the video, but not everything she wanted could be done. As MTV's Vineyard reported, Lindsay wanted to break the mirror in the bathroom for the video, but an assistant director on set tried to talk her out of it. 'This is real glass, Lindsay. We weren't prepared for you to break these things.' (In the end, they decided it was OK for her to crack, but not shatter, the mirror).

'I actually did cry at the end [when recording the song]', she told Vineyard. 'It was very emotional. Kara kept saying, "Do it once more," and I was like, "I can't do it!" and then I broke down and ran into the bathroom and closed the door. A lot of the stuff in the video has happened in my real life.'

'As glamorous as this life looks,' she added, 'it's not always. I had a lot of personal things going on, and my life was out of order. I needed to take control of what was going on. I feel like the past year has been a whirlwind, and I've just grown up so much.'

Certainly, the crew on the video shoot were impressed with Lindsay's professionalism. 'Lindsay knows what she wants,' actor Drake told MTV. 'There's no beating around the bush. She's patient and she's calm, and she gets her points across very clearly.'

The video's director of photography, Jim Hawkinson, also praised Lindsay. 'Some directors are control freaks,' he said. 'She's not. She trusts us to give her what she wants. And that's the most important thing in being a director – knowing what you want. In this case, she wanted a controversial video that would make a statement, that would let her vent, that would show that her life is a fishbowl.'

Tommy Mottola added: 'This song, this video, this album, are going to show that she's a serious artist. She's not just a teen Hollywood actress playing around with a singing career. This will show what she's capable of. And I bet you she'll get offered more jobs as a director than as an actress.' Lindsay laughed at his suggestion. 'I would consider directing again, my next video,' she told Vineyard. 'Maybe a happy song next time, though.'

Of course, one thing that must have been on her mind was how her father would react to the song. 'I hope he'll see what I say in the song is, "I love you" so many times, that I need him, and he'll see the crazy things in my life. I hope he sees the positive side of the video rather than the negative. The video is kind of offensive, but it is very raw. He's my father. I need someone to walk me down the aisle when I get married,' she said to *OK!* magazine. In response, Michael wrote an open letter to Lindsay via the *New York Daily News*. 'While I always considered and expressed how truly blessed Lindsay, as well as my other children are, I never realised how blessed I am to have a daughter as amazing as Lindsay,' he said in the letter. 'Hold onto my shirt, honey, soon enough you'll be able to hold onto me! While the media and press love to cover Lindsay enjoying her life and successes, hopefully now they will cover the kind of heart this beautiful and gifted young lady really has.'

He also revealed that he was writing his own song in response to his daughter's song. Called 'A Father's Love', he wrote it in prison after hearing Lindsay's song, but didn't reveal it to the world until 2007 (he later announced in 2010 he wanted to release it as a single). The tune appeared on the Internet, and was sung by an unnamed friend. It seemed Lindsay's relationship with her father was destined to be forever in the press. Meanwhile, she had had the therapy of writing about her life for the album, as she told MTV in 2005: 'I've been writing a lot, almost every night. There's been a lot going on [in my life lately], and people can find that escape in hobbies that they do. I don't do yoga or anything, but some people use that. Everyone has their own thing, and I use writing.'

It certainly made *A Little More Personal (Raw)* a fascinating album that was almost an autobiography in song. Though she included two cover versions – 'I Want You To Want Me', originally by Cheap Trick, and 'Edge Of Seventeen', written and originally recorded by Stevie Nicks – the rest of Lindsay's album was filled with songs that suited her and her life.

Released on 6 December 2005 in the US, the album featured a photo of Lindsay on the cover, looking over her shoulder with her bare back to the camera, and a Chinese symbol in red across it (the symbol means 'raw' and also 'living'). Reviews for the album were mixed. *Rolling Stone* gave it just two stars out of five, with reviewer Brian Hiatt writing that 'Lohan has a much bigger – though less distinctive – voice than her sometime-pal Ashlee Simpson, but she sounds like a high-school talent-show winner on the album's two classic-rock covers.' PopMatters.com added that: 'For the most part, *A Little More Personal* oscillates between dull ballads, bad covers and interchangeable guitar-driven stabs at emulating Kelly Clarkson's acclaimed "Since U Been Gone".'

It was not all bad news, however. *Entertainment Weekly* graded the album a B-minus, and commented that 'Lohan's (admittedly studio-sheened) brand of pop darkness reads realer than Ashlee Simpson's', and All-Music.com's Stephen Thomas Erlewine wrote about the album: 'It is an intriguing mash-up of heart and commerce. And it does suggest one thing that [her first album] *Speak* never did: Lindsay Lohan may have an artistic vision as a recording artist, which is indeed a huge step forward.'

As 2005 came to an end, Lindsay even had plans to tour Taiwan, after learning her first album had achieved gold status there. 'I would love to [tour Taiwan],' she told reporters at the launch of *A Little More Personal*. 'I haven't toured at all at this point, but I would really love to do that. It's a great feeling to know that people in other places and other countries are aware of my music and what I do.'

The tour didn't happen in the end, but that didn't stop the early months of 2006 from being eventful. On New Year's Eve, Lindsay hosted a party at Prive Nightclub in Miami, even taking a turn as DJ during the evening. However, her stay in Miami ended up with her being hospitalised at the Miami Mount Sinai Medical Center on Monday 2 January, following an asthma attack. She remained in hospital for two days before being taken back to New York by her mother. 'It's the first attack since I've known her,' Lindsay's publicist Leslie Sloane Zelnik said in a statement. 'She's had attacks before, but not that many, and not recently. She's taking it easy now, she's resting comfortably. She's just tired, and not feeling too good. It took a lot out of her.'

Then, as Lindsay was recuperating that week, she made headlines again with a revealing interview she had given to *Vanity Fair*. Accompanied by stunning photos of a bleached-blond Lindsay on a California beach, the interview featured Lindsay talking about her relationship with her parents, her album and the various rumours that surrounded her life, from her hospital stay during the filming of *Herbie: Fully Loaded* to her relationship with Wilmer Valderrama. However, the comments from the feature that made headlines around the world were more controversial. During the interview, journalist Evgenia Peretz quoted Lindsay as saying 'I was making myself sick', which Peretz interpreted as 'bulimic episodes'. On 11 January, a few days after the *Vanity Fair* issue, with Lindsay on the cover, appeared on the newsstands, Lindsay released a statement to *Teen People*.

'The words that I gave to the writer for *Vanity Fair* were misused and misconstrued, and I'm appalled with the way it was done. Aside from [the writer's] lies and changing of my words, I am blessed to have this job and the wonderful family I do.'

Vanity Fair, however, stood by their article. In a statement, they said: 'Evgenia Peretz is one of our most reliable reporters. Every word Lindsay Lohan told her is on tape. *Vanity Fair* stands by the story.

Lindsay's mother Dina also commented on the story, telling *People*: 'In the other parts of the article, it's a girl growing up who had a really crappy year, and wants other kids to know, "Don't be suicidal, don't be stupid, you'll make it through." That was her message, and hopefully girls will get that. I believe honesty prevails.'

Lindsay didn't have much time to dwell on the *Vanity Fair* interview. She was filming her next movie, *Chapter 27*, and spending time with her friends, including Kelly Osbourne and Paris Hilton. And, after stays at the Four Seasons and Beverly Hills Hotels, she was now living at the Chateau Marmont Hotel, one of Hollywood's most famous – and infamous – hostelries.

The Chateau Marmont is an eye-catching hotel that is part of Hollywood legend. Nestled behind trees on Sunset Boulevard, it was built in 1927 and is loosely modelled on the Chateau D'Amboise in the Loire Valley in France. Originally an apartment building when it opened in 1929, it became a hotel in 1931. As well as the main building, the hotel boasts four bungalows for its guests, many of whom stay for months and years rather than for a short holiday. Keanu Reeves made it his home until 2003, and Vivien Leigh lived there after her split from husband Laurence Olivier, but it is more famous for the many notorious events that have happened behind the hotel's walls. Jim Morrison of The Doors hurt his back while hanging from a drainpipe after trying to climb into his room via the window;

members of Led Zeppelin drove their motorbikes through the lobby and Jean Harlow is rumoured to have slept with Clark Gable in one of the suites while on her honeymoon with Harold Rosson.

The most famous incident at the Chateau Marmont, however, is also one of the saddest.

In 1982 comedian John Belushi, star of classic movies including *National Lampoon's Animal House* and *The Blues Brothers*, was living in one of the hotel bungalows. Born in 1949 in Chicago, John Belushi rose to fame in 1975 when he joined the cast of *Saturday Night Live* – the comedy show Lindsay would herself present three decades later. He became known for his impersonations of celebrities including Henry Kissinger, Elvis, Marlon Brando and even John Lennon, and for his original characters such as Samurai Futaba and Jacob Papageorge (otherwise known as 'Joliet' Jake Blues). He appeared each week alongside such stars as Dan Aykroyd, Bill Murray and Chevy Chase, becoming a household name. However, it was a movie role – in *National Lampoon's Animal House*, released in 1978 – that truly made John an international star, as fans around the world fell in love with his character John 'Bluto' Blutarsky, a partying student at Faber College who creates havoc (including an infamous food fight) wherever he goes. The film made over $120 million in the US alone – it was the second most popular movie that year, after *Grease* – and has since been voted one of the best movie comedies of all time.

However, behind the scenes, all was not well with John Belushi. He had a drink and drugs problem that he had tried to control during filming by staying with his wife, rather than the cast and crew, who were together in a hotel. 'They [the producers] wanted to keep John away because they knew his tendencies. So they got him and [his wife] Judy a house in the suburbs,' co-star Tim Matheson told *Entertainment Weekly* in a look back at the movie, while director John Landis added: 'John was clean. And he was working hard because he saw this movie as a big opportunity. When we did *Blues Brothers*, later, he had a very bad cocaine habit. On *Animal House* that wasn't true.'

His movie career took off with *Animal House*, and the following year John left *Saturday Night Live* to work solely on movies. He made the quirky comedy *1941* for director Steven Spielberg, and in 1980 he reteamed with pal Dan Aykroyd and director John Landis for the comedy *The Blues Brothers*. Based on their *SNL* characters, the movie has become a cult classic. Belushi played 'Joliet' Jake Blues, freshly paroled from prison (where he had served three years for armed robbery) while Aykroyd played his brother, Elwood, who collects him from jail in a battered police car (the Bluesmobile). The pair discover their old home, a Roman Catholic orphanage, is about to be closed, so they decide to reform their band, The Blues Brothers, in order to raise the cash to save it.

Featuring a memorable car chase, supporting performances from Carrie Fisher, John Candy and even Steven Spielberg, the movie also boasted a *Who's Who* of musical acts among its cast – Aretha Franklin, Ray Charles, James Brown and Chaka Khan among them. It was another hit – one of the most successful musicals of all time, with a bestselling soundtrack, too.

Belushi was a megastar. He made more movies – *Neighbours* and *Continental Divide*, which were less successful than his previous films – but the one everyone was excited about was a science-fiction comedy called *Ghostbusters*. John was due to play Dr Peter Venkman in the movie, alongside Dan Aykroyd and Harold Ramis, who wrote the movie, but he did not live to see the movie made (it was made, of course, in 1984, with Bill Murray replacing John in the role of Venkman).

In March 1982, John was living at the Chateau Marmont in Bungalow 3. On the evening of 5 March, Robin Williams and Robert De Niro had been among the friends who had popped by for a visit, and after they left, John had other friends in the room, including a woman named Cathy Smith. It was Cathy who later admitted giving John drugs, including speedballs (a mixture of heroin and cocaine) before leaving in the early morning. A few hours later, Bill Wallace, a friend of John, entered the bungalow when no one answered his knock. He found John lying in bed. He was confirmed dead by paramedics at 12.45 p.m. Four days later, medical examiner Dr Kornblum concluded in his autopsy that 'John Belushi, a thirty-three-year-old white male, died of acute toxicity from cocaine and heroin'. An extremely talented man had died, and a Hollywood legend – set at the Chateau Marmont hotel – was born.

As Columbia Pictures founder Harry Cohn said many years before, in 1939: 'If you must get in trouble, do it at the Chateau Marmont.'

Getting in trouble wasn't new resident Lindsay Lohan's intention, of course. Lindsay was staying in a suite described by *Allure*'s Deanna Kizis as 'more like an apartment, with a full kitchen, living room and dining room that Lohan has turned into a 330-square-foot closet. Around the large oak dining table are three clothing racks that are chock-full of designer pieces – all part of Lohan's personal and ever-expanding collection.'

'I love to shop,' Lindsay told Kizis, who went on to write that Lindsay had just returned from the Dior boutique in Beverly Hills, where she and pal Kelly Osbourne bought matching pairs of gigantic rhinestone sunglasses. In the interview, she also told Kizis how she felt about her career ('I hate it when people call me a teen queen'), her weight ('Sometimes being that thin doesn't look healthy. I kind of didn't realise that'), and how she was feeling following a traumatic 2005: 'I feel like I've lived five lifetimes because I've grown up a lot,' she said. 'I know better what to do and what not to do. I lost sight of the people and things that are most important to me.'

Chateau Marmont was, at least for a while, home. But Lindsay wasn't there that much as, when spring came to Los Angeles in 2006, she also had two movies she had made in 2005 ready for release that had to be promoted with interviews, photo shoots and TV appearances. First was the comedy *Just My Luck*, formerly known as the 'Luck Project', which she had filmed in the summer of 2005. Directed by Donald Petrie, who had made box-office hits *Miss Congeniality* and *How to Lose A Guy In 10 Days*, the movie was Lindsay's first 'grown-up' romantic comedy. She co-starred with Chris Pine, now better known as a young James Kirk in 2009's *Star Trek*, and *The O.C.*'s Samaire Armstrong.

In an interview with journalist Paul Fischer, Lindsay chatted about the role being different from anything she had done before. 'It's like a coming-of-age thing for me, and everything that I'm doing after this, my characters are the same age if not older, and maturing. You can only act as if you're in high school for so long, I feel. It's not a dark film, so I can still keep the fan base that I've grown with. It's a really lovely film and it's my first romantic comedy, and I get to kiss Chris [Pine] in it. It's a great film for me, it still has a good message, and that's important.'

She added: 'I still have a young audience to look out for, and this is acceptable for the younger audience, and for people that are older than me. It was hard for me to find that kind of film, so it was nice that I found it.'

As the title makes obvious, the movie is all about luck. Lindsay plays Ashley Albright, a young woman who has always been very lucky. Jake Hardin (Pine), meanwhile, is followed by bad luck wherever he goes. Their lives intertwine at a masquerade party Ashley organises: Jake, who manages a band called McFly (yes, the real British pop band, here playing a less successful version of themselves), hatches a plan to attend so he can meet an influential figure in the music industry who could help him.

At the party, a fortune-teller tells Ashley her luck is about to change for the worse. She and Jake, both wearing masks, so unaware of who the other is, share a kiss, and Ashley's good luck transfers to Jake while his rotten luck goes to her. Before long, Jake gets McFly signed to a major record label while Ashley finds herself in jail. Determined to get her good luck back, she visits the fortune-teller, who says the only way to return things to normal is to kiss the person she kissed before. Of course, Ashley doesn't know who that is, but even if she does find out it is Jake, will she kiss him and ruin his life, or let him keep his good luck?

Interviewer Paul Fischer of Girl.com.au asked Lindsay about her own luck when he talked to her about the movie, and whether she felt as if she had ever had her own streak of bad luck. 'If I did, I didn't know about it,' Lindsay replied. 'You have to go through highs and lows in life to learn to appreciate things, just as Ashley does in the movie.'

Unfortunately for Lindsay, there were more lows than highs on the immediate horizon. *Just My Luck* opened in cinemas on 12 May 2006, and was not greeted with rave reviews. The *Rotten Tomatoes* website called it a 'screwball romcom that fails to take advantage of Lindsay Lohan's considerable charm', *Empire* said the film had 'occasional funny moments' but was 'very, very thin', and Roger Ebert of the *Chicago Sun-Times* said 'it's safe, competent and bland'. Even the bad reviews, however, singled Lindsay out for praise – Matthew Turner of *View London* mentioning her 'comic timing and self-deprecating charm', and *Entertainment Weekly* commenting that 'even in her dullest vehicle, Lindsay Lohan exudes an unfake-able shine'.

Lindsay wasn't just being critiqued for her movie performance, however. In May 2006 she became the subject of a row that blazed over the internet. According to culture blogger Dawn Olsen, Lindsay was partying at the Los Angeles club Hyde, as was Paris Hilton. Apparently the two argued, but it didn't end there. Paris, along with friends including millionaire heir Brandon Davis, videoed themselves on a cell phone saying offensive things about Lindsay and their words were circulated online. Olsen notes: 'The frenzied verbal abuse reaches its crescendo about Lindsay's wealth, or lack thereof.' 'I think she's worth about seven million [dollars], which means she's really poor. It's disgusting. She lives in a motel, in New York,' Davis says.

It was a nasty, foul, offensive rant, and Paris Hilton's publicist Elliot Mintz was quick to release a statement about his client's involvement. 'The only thing I want to underscore is that the person making the statements was not Paris Hilton. It is unfair to characterise Brandon's statements as being reflective of Paris's feelings about Lindsay. We're dealing with two different people. It was Brandon who was speaking, and of course there are moments when Paris was laughing, but she never said anything. Brandon was speaking for himself, not for her. Personally, I found the incident unnecessary.'

Davis also issued an apology on 26 May. 'My behaviour on 16 May was inexcusable,' he said in a statement. 'What started out as a joke got completely carried away, and I am horrified at the words that came out of my mouth. I consider Lindsay a friend, and I hope she accepts my sincere apology for my reprehensible actions last week.'

By 6 June, it seemed the matter was settled. Lindsay's publicist, Leslie Sloane Zelnik told the *New York Post*: 'Lindsay took the high road and accepted Brandon's apology last week.' In an interview with *Harper's Bazaar*, Lindsay's mother Dina also commented on the horrid incident. 'I know Brandon. I know his mother. A beautiful woman. You know, if her son went off and went dark? Whatever he did, he did, and it was bad and it was disgusting,' she said. 'He doesn't have a dad who was always there. I don't judge someone until I walk in his shoes. His mother was hurt by his father.

My ex did that to me. And what does that do to a kid? That hurts him. So how does he have a relationship?'

There was a bright spot on the horizon for Lindsay, however. In the summer of 2005 she had been asked to appear in legendary director Robert Altman's latest project, *A Prairie Home Companion*, and on 9 June 2006, the movie was to be released. It was an honour to appear in an Altman movie. Eighty years old at the time *Prairie* was made, he had had a distinguished career in Hollywood following his hiring at CBS TV in 1957 to work on the series *Alfred Hitchcock Presents*. He followed this with directorial work on shows such as *Maverick*, *Bonanza* and *Route 66*, but made his name when he directed the movie *M*A*S*H* in 1969, a film that won the Grand Prix at the Cannes Film Festival in 1970 and was also nominated for six Academy Awards, including Best Director (it won only one, Best Screenplay).

More acclaimed movies followed for Altman, including *McCabe & Mrs Miller* with Warren Beatty and Julie Christie, *The Long Goodbye* with Elliot Gould, and 1975's *Nashville*, for which he was again nominated for an Academy Award. While his success waned in the 1980s (Altman directed the Robin Williams-starring *Popeye*, which was a career low for both of them), his career was revitalised in 1992 when he directed the Hollywood satire *The Player*. Stars including Julia Roberts, Bruce Willis, Whoopi Goldberg, John Cusack, Susan Sarandon, Jack Lemmon and Anjelica Huston lined up to have brief cameo roles in the movie that later won Altman the BAFTA for Best Director and a similar award at the Cannes Film Festival. Everyone wanted to work for the great director, and, since *The Player,* many have, including Julianne Moore, Robert Downey Jr and Matthew Modine (1993's *Short Cuts*), Sophia Loren, Marcello Mastroianni and Kim Basinger (1994's *Prêt-à-Porter*), Helen Mirren, Maggie Smith, Eileen Atkins, Alan Bates and Michael Gambon (2001's *Gosford Park,* which won Altman another Oscar nomination).

For *A Prairie Home Companion*, Lindsay would not only be directed by a great, talented man, but she would also be sharing the screen with another collection of terrific actors and actresses that he had assembled. The ensemble comedy would include in its cast such names as Woody Harrelson, Tommy Lee Jones, Kevin Kline, John C. Reilly, writer Garrison Keillor and none other than Meryl Streep. In fact, Lindsay's role was to play Oscar-winner Streep's daughter.

In an interview for About.com, Lindsay talked about how the role came about. 'I wasn't aware of exactly what it [*A Prairie Home Companion*, the radio show] was. I spoke to my grandmother about it and she informed me what it was about. The movie was coming together, and I heard Meryl Streep's name, then I heard Michelle Pfeiffer at one point, and then it finally just happened one day. They said, 'OK, we're making the movie, and they want you to be Meryl Streep's daughter in it.' Would you turn down a movie that Robert Altman was directing and Meryl Streep was playing your mother in?'

It was a daunting role that, as *Vanity Fair* reported in early 2006, required Lindsay to sing, improvise and learn scenes that were twenty-five pages long. 'I was *scared*,' she told the magazine about the first day of shooting in Minnesota, when she had to perform a long scene with Streep and Lily Tomlin as her character's aunt. 'Meryl and Lily are singing this emotional song and I'm chiming in. And I don't have a father in the movie, I don't really know my dad. And she's talking about the dad and she starts singing, and I just started to cry in the scene when we were improvising . . . they keep rolling and then all of a sudden Meryl starts crying, Lily starts crying. The crew members start tearing up . . . We cut. Robert Altman starts clapping and everyone starts clapping. Meryl starts clapping. And they start coming up to me and saying, "That was amazing, I can't believe it wasn't scripted." It was so beautiful. That was the first day of shooting . . . They were so nice to me and kind, and I was so proud of myself. That changed me a lot, I guess.'

Altman spoke to *Vanity Fair* about filming with Lindsay. 'She has to do a song which is not very good – her character's performance is not very good – and yet it had to be honest, so it couldn't be tricked. She was excellent.'

In fact, Lindsay did so well her role was actually made larger, as she told About.com. 'My role kind of got bigger as we went along because I became friends with [writer] Garrison Keillor,' she explained. 'It was amazing. I would look at the call sheet and I would just see these actors that I didn't believe were coming onto the set every day. It was a wonderful experience, and good experience for me as my first independent film. It was nice to be able to sing live, and it's just one of those movies where it's always nice to have to look back on. It's an amazing, monumental film – and cast – in its own way.'

The movie was based on a public radio show of the same name, written by Garrison Keillor, who also starred as himself in the movie. While the radio show was Keillor talking about his day-to-day experiences, the movie had a fictional story tied around the show – imagining what was going on behind the scenes. The characters who performed for the variety show included singing and guitar-playing cowboys Dusty (Woody Harrelson) and Lefty (John C. Reilly), and the Johnson sisters – Rhonda (Tomlin) and Yolanda (Streep) – who constantly bicker, while Yolanda is also trying to convince her shy daughter Lola (Lindsay) to sing on the last show. While this is going on, a woman in a white coat wanders around the theatre, and the show's security guard, Guy Noir (Kevin Kline), follows her.

Lindsay was surrounded by talented actors on set, many of whom had been in the business much longer than she had, and to make her even more nervous, she had to sing the song 'Frankie And Johnny' in the film.

'I was definitely nervous,' she told About.com. 'Everybody was on set that day. On that day, they just happened to have to be there on the side of the stage. I only rehearsed that song I think three times, and they kept changing it. I was nervous.'

She added: 'We don't really have musicals that are done like this movie. And Robert Altman obviously has a way of incorporating comedy and the darker side in films. It's kind of a creepy movie in its own way, but still it's really funny.'

Her co-star Meryl Streep jumped at the chance to praise her. 'I don't think she's any darker than any of the other teens that I'm close to,' Meryl Streep told journalist Rebecca Murray when asked about Lindsay and whether she was like her dark character, Lola, in the movie. 'It's very easy to feel motherly towards her, and in fact, she is younger than three of my kids. I feel it's so hard for these young actors. I mean, she turned nineteen on our movie. It's a different world that they're coming up in, and there is so much money to be made off of their personal lives. People are bound and determined to make that money, and I felt protective of her. I felt bad that this is the world that we've given this generation of kids.'

Meryl also defended Lindsay in an interview with *W*, when asked about her co-star's partying image. 'She's very young. It's a wonderful time in somebody's life. I'm aware of the tabloid stuff because my kids tell me – but I don't read it, and frankly, I couldn't care less. When they say "action", Lindsay is completely, visibly living in front of the camera, and that's all anybody really cares about.'

Lindsay and Meryl became friends on set, too. 'It was more of a "friends" relationship,' Lindsay told Murray. 'Her daughters were there all the time and one is my age, one is older and one's younger. They're really sweet. The whole cast went to dinner every single night. We had nothing else, really, to do, so everyone really got close with each other. It was like a big family, which is really amazing.'

The finished movie was first shown to the press at the South By Southwest Film Festival on 10 March, and then opened in cinemas two months later. It was met with good reviews. Roger Ebert of the *Chicago Sun-Times* said: 'What a lovely film this is, so gentle and whimsical, so simple and profound,' while *Rolling Stone* said that director Altman 'brings out the best in Lindsay Lohan as Yolanda's daughter Lola, who writes suicide poetry. Lohan rises to the occasion, delivering a rock-the-house version of "Frankie And Johnny".'

Despite some ups and downs earlier in the year, Lindsay now had something to celebrate. She was almost twenty years old, and had had the opportunity to work with both a legendary Hollywood director and an Oscar-winning cast (Streep, Kline and Tommy Lee Jones had all won Academy Awards), something few of her contemporaries could boast. But as always in Lindsay's life, there were rougher times to come . . .

Chapter Seven
This Too Shall Pass

As summer 2006 began, Lindsay was busy filming *Georgia Rule* in towns such as Santa Clarita and Santa Paula on the Californian coast. It was another grown-up movie for her, directed by Garry Marshall, who had made such hits as *Beaches*, *Pretty Woman* and *The Princess Diaries*. And it was another terrific cast, too, as Lindsay was starring alongside Felicity Huffman (best known for her role as Lynette Scavo in *Desperate Housewives*), Cary Elwes of *Saw* and *The Princess Bride* fame, *My Best Friend's Wedding*'s Dermot Mulroney and, most impressive of all, acclaimed actress Jane Fonda.

The daughter of legendary screen star Henry Fonda, Jane – like Lindsay – also grew up in the spotlight. She became a tabloid sensation when she protested against the Vietnam War, and was photographed sitting on a north Vietnamese anti-aircraft gun (which earned her the nickname Hanoi Jane). She was also an accomplished actress, who made her screen debut aged twenty-three, and carved out a career that included memorable roles in movies such as 1965 comedy western *Cat Ballou*, romantic comedy *Barefoot In the Park* with Robert Redford, and two distinctive roles she will always be associated with: as Barbarella in the 1968 sci-fi fantasy of the same name, and prostitute Bree in the 1971 thriller *Klute*. Jane starred alongside Vanessa Redgrave in *Julia*, Michael Douglas in *The China Syndrome* and both her father and Katherine Hepburn in *On Golden Pond*. She also won Best Actress Oscars for *Klute* and *Coming Home*, and then took a break from acting in 1991, returning in 2005 to co-star with Jennifer Lopez in *Monster-in-Law*, to which *Georgia Rule* was her follow-up movie.

Jane talked about working with Lindsay on the movie to journalist Kam Williams. 'She has an ability to access her emotions that's very beautiful. She's made me cry several times when I'm giving her the off-stage lines. She's made me cry, and she's very moving.'

Unfortunately, because *Georgia Rule* was filmed within driving distance of Lindsay's hotel home in Los Angeles, she was often photographed in nightclubs after a day's filming. Matters came to a head, however, when on 26 July, *People* reported that Lindsay had been hospitalised early that morning. 'She was overheated and dehydrated,' Lindsay's publicist told *The Insider* TV show, who were first to report on the incident. 'She was filming in 105-degree weather for twelve hours.'

People went on to report that: 'A friend of the actress tells *People* that prior to her hospitalisation, Lohan was at the Chateau Marmont and then the nightclub Guy's. Confirms an observer at Guy's: "She was definitely partying. She wasn't over the top, but having a great time." Another Lohan pal tells *People* the actress has been "shooting in 120-degree weather. She told me it was hotter than when she was shooting in the *Herbie: Fully Loaded* fire suit."'

People went on to report that Lindsay spent several hours in the hospital, where she was given a Vitamin B shot before being sent home. The incident had far-reaching consequences. James G. Robinson, the head of Morgan Creek Productions, who were making the movie, wrote a letter to Lindsay that was made public (it was posted on thesmokinggun.com) on 28 July.

The letter, dated 26 July, callenged her reasons for her absences from the *Georgia Rule* set: 'You and your representatives have told us that your various late arrivals and absences from the set have been the result of illness; today we were told it was 'heat exhaustion'. We are well aware that your ongoing all-night heavy partying is the real reason for your so-called "exhaustion".' The letter went on to issue an ultimatum: 'If you do not honour your production commitments . . .

we will hold you personally accountable. This means that in addition to pursuing full monetary damages, we will take such other action as we deem necessary to preserve the integrity of the *Georgia Rule* production as well as Morgan Creek's financial interests.'

In an interview with *The Hollywood Reporter* days after the letter went public, Robinson said: 'I'm just trying to get the movie made. I did what I felt I needed to do on behalf of the movie, and on behalf of her, too. I wanted to set some limits. It was not a nasty letter. It was, "Come on, be a professional." We're halfway through [filming] with six weeks to go. There's no turning back. I wrote the letter; it was from me, not some damn attorney. She showed up. That's all I cared about.'

When the movie was released almost a year later, Robinson talked again about the letter he had sent Lindsay. 'I wrote that letter six times. I started out being pissed off. There was anger in some drafts, but I think I accomplished what I wanted to accomplish. And from that day on, she didn't miss any time. She came to work on time, knew her lines and boy, she's a fantastic actor. She's probably one of the most talented.'

The director of *Georgia Rule*, Garry Marshall, told press at the movie's première that the letter had been his idea. 'Once somebody walks on my set, it's my problem, but we can't go chasing them. This film is low-budget. We can't lose days . . . Tough love is a part of this business – she missed a day on the second week of shooting. Jim wrote the memo, and she came the next day and we were fine.'

Jane Fonda also commented on Lindsay's life in September 2006, when she was interviewed by TV show *Access Hollywood*. 'Every once in a while, a very, very young person who is burning both ends of the candle needs to have somebody say, "You know, you're going to pay the piper. You better slow down." So I think it [the letter] was good.

'[Lohan's] in the magazines, so you always know what she's doing because you can just read about it in the tabloids,' Jane Fonda added. 'She parties all the time … And you know, she's young and she can get away with it. But it's hard after a while to party very hard and work very hard. She'll learn that.

'I just want to take her in my arms and hold her until she becomes grown up. She's so young, and she's so alone out there in the world in terms of structure and, you know, people to nurture her. And she's so talented.'

Happily, the rest of the production on *Georgia Rule* went smoothly. The story was a comedy drama in which Lindsay plays rebellious teen Rachel, with whom her mother Lily (Huffman) has lost all patience. She decides the only person who can handle Rachel is Lily's mother, Georgia (Fonda), so Lily literally drags Rachel into her car to take her there for an enforced stay. Georgia has strict rules she expects her granddaughter to follow, and Rachel resists but eventually settles down a little, even getting a job with the local vet (and unofficial doctor of the town), Simon (Dermot Mulroney).

Rachel also meets young Harlan (Garrett Hedlund), a Mormon boy her age who admits to her that he's a virgin. Rachel ends up giving him oral sex, and then the pair drive to see Harlan's girlfriend so he can admit what he's done. Meanwhile, Rachel is in trouble with both her mother and grandmother. Under pressure, she reveals the real reason she has been such a troublemaker in recent years – since the age of twelve she has been molested by her mother's new husband, Arnold (Cary Elwes). However, Lily doesn't believe her, and it is only her grandmother Georgia who thinks she is telling the truth.

The movie was an odd mix of drama and comedy and, when it was released in May 2007, it didn't receive great reviews. *The Village Voice* newspaper in New York called it 'an incoherent dramedy', *Time Out* called the movie 'unforgivable' and the *Los Angeles Times* said 'it oscillates clumsily from shock to slapstick to schmaltz'.

However, Lindsay did receive praise for her performance, with *The Village Voice*'s Ella Taylor writing: 'A self-possessed, intelligent screen presence, she can outgun almost any caricature, including a parody of herself … [Her movie character] stays out late, lies – maybe – through her teeth and creates mayhem. So, yes, *Georgia Rule* might profitably be retitled *The Lindsay Lohan*

Story, but peeking out from all the strutting and preening is a strong, decent person in the making. With luck, that same person may yet rise up to deliver Lohan – whose well-documented freak-out occurred on the set of *Georgia Rule* – from her off-screen antics.'

Richard Roeper of the *Chicago Sun-Times* also singled her out for praise, saying: 'It's a shame Lohan's best work to date is bogged down in a film that wants to be in the same league as *Terms of Endearment* but is only marginally better than *Divine Secrets of the Ya-Ya Sisterhood*.'

This acclaim for Lindsay came a year after she had made tabloid headlines following the letter by James G. Robinson appearing in the press. Lindsay spoke about the incident, in a 2007 interview with *Allure*. 'It upset me because I was … a bit irresponsible. I didn't think about the consequences, but I was also going through something in my life.'

That 'something' was a three-month relationship with Harry Morton. Harry is the son of Peter Morton, the co-founder of the Hard Rock Café, which began as a one-off restaurant featuring rock 'n' roll memorabilia near London's Hyde Park in 1971. Since then, Hard Rock has grown into a chain of theme restaurants around the world, and even a hotel, the Hard Rock Hotel & Casino in Las Vegas. In 1995, Morton sold the restaurants for a reported $410 million, making son Harry (who owns his own LA restaurant, Pink Taco, and, more recently, the nightclub The Viper Room) a very wealthy heir.

As soon as Lindsay's relationship with Harry became public on 2 July, it was splashed all over the tabloids. *People* reported that 'their relationship started out promisingly: they spent a cosy Fourth of July week in Malibu lounging at Morton's pad (where they blasted Led Zeppelin over the speakers), dining at Nobu, shopping at the Malibu Country Mart and going out with pals. By mid-month, the lovebirds were nearly inseparable. Among their many outings: holding hands at the Prada party in Beverly Hills on 13 July, hitting hotspot Les Deux with pal Nicole Richie on 14 July and celebrating David Spade's birthday together on 15 July. Morton was on the scene when Lindsay was briefly hospitalised on 26 July (her camp blamed dehydration and exhaustion), and subsequently missed work on her upcoming drama *Georgia Rule*.'

Lindsay did joke early on in the relationship, to World Entertainment News Network, that Morton was actually her third choice of man. 'My favourite is Johnny Depp, but he's married, isn't he? And sadly, Ashton Kutcher is taken, too!'

In August, the press speculated that Harry was going to propose to Lindsay after he was seen shopping in jewellery store Cartier, and then the couple were photographed hugging and kissing on 3 September 2006, on holiday in Maui. But by 22 September, *People* reported the pair had split. Reporter Carrie Borzillo-Vrenna wrote: '"Harry broke up with Lindsay yesterday at Chateau Marmont after they had dinner on the courtyard patio," a source tells *People*. "Nothing happened at dinner, but shortly afterward, he broke up with her." Why the split? "She was too much drama," says a source close to Harry. "Lindsay did cut down on the partying, but with her it's all relative. Harry is sober. It wasn't the partying that broke them up. Harry's more low-key, and not into the same stuff she's into." However, the Lohan pal says, "No one 'dumped' anyone. You don't dump people when you're twenty and twenty-five. You have a mature relationship, and you take a break and you see what happens. Everyone does that.'"

The day after the story ran, Lindsay's representative stated that 'the story is untrue', while Morton's representative added: 'I do not comment on his personal life.'

Three years after their relationship ended, Morton did comment, when he discussed having a romance under the media spotlight in an interview with *Inked* magazine. 'It is the worst thing of all time … I'll be happy if it never happens again,' he said of appearing on tabloid covers. In the same interview, he even denied dating Lindsay in the first place – despite there being numerous photos of the couple together (including those of them kissing in Maui) that prove otherwise. 'I didn't really date her,' he said. 'This is one of those things where people will say, "Yes, you did." But I really didn't. Don't believe everything that you read. You hang out with someone for, like, one week and they can extend that for, like, two months' worth of pictures. It's more embarrassing being known for that. I'd like to be known for stuff I've created or things I've done. I don't want to be known for that. No way.'

It's fair to guess that Lindsay didn't want to be known for her personal life, either. While tabloids reported whom she was seen out with (and at home with – snaps had even been taken of Lindsay and Harry on a private balcony at his own home), Lindsay was still making movies, including two based on real events – *Chapter 27* and *Bobby*.

Bobby, which was filmed at the end of 2005 and the start of 2006, was the first to be released, having premiered at the Venice Film Festival in September 2006 (an event Lindsay attended with then beau Harry Morton) before being released in the US on 17 November. It was an ensemble movie featuring an impressive cast: Harry Belafonte, Laurence Fishburne, Anthony Hopkins, Helen Hunt, *Fringe*'s Joshua Jackson, Shia LaBeouf, Ashton Kutcher and real-life wife Demi Moore, Martin Sheen, Christian Slater, Sharon Stone and *The Lord of the Rings'* Elijah Wood all shared the screen while the director (who also had a small role in the movie and wrote the script) was actor Emilio Estevez.

The movie, a fictional account of events leading up to Senator Robert Kennedy's death in 1968, was a subject close to Estevez's heart. The actor, best known for his roles in *The Breakfast Club* and *Young Guns*, told Canadian journalist Sheila Roberts in an interview that he remembered as a six-year-old hearing that Kennedy had been shot at the Ambassador Hotel in Los Angeles, and running to wake his father, actor Martin Sheen, with the news. Weeks later his father took him to visit the hotel. 'I remember my dad holding my hand as we wandered through those grand halls, and I remembered my father talking about what we had lost,' Estevez told Roberts. 'From that moment of 5 June 1968 on, it seemed we became more and more cynical and resigned, and I think it's a big part of why we are where we are at culturally today,' he added. 'It's heartbreaking.'

He also talked about what a labour of love it was to get the movie made. One of the problems was that the Ambassador Hotel, where Kennedy was shot, was due to be demolished. Estevez got only five days to film there with his starry cast. 'The circumstances were extreme,' he told Roberts. 'They were tearing it down around us, and there were some shots where, if you were to widen out, you would actually see the bulldozers working, and the agreement was that they would not stop demolition while we were there. Didn't matter if we were in the middle of a dialogue scene because they worked around the clock, 24/7 Monday through Sunday. To get those five days and to have the actors stand on that hallowed ground ... I think they carried that sentiment with them to every location that we used after the fact to cobble the hotel together.' (The hotel was completely demolished by January 2006, and schools now stand on the famous site.)

The role that Lindsay was to play in the movie, Diane, was actually one of the first to take shape when Estevez was struggling to write the script. He told Urban Cinefile in an interview that, while suffering from writer's block, he checked into a motel in California's Pismo Beach and was recognised by the female receptionist. 'She asked what I was doing up there, and I said I'm writing a script about the day Bobby Kennedy was shot,' remembered Estevez. 'She nearly fell over. Her eyes rolled up and she said, "I was there!"'

'She broke my writer's block, and I wrote that character [Diane] with her permission, and incorporated her into the piece,' said Estevez. 'When the shots broke out Diane said it was as if the rug was pulled out from underneath her entire generation.' The real-life Diane – not her real first name – went on to marry two men in order to keep them from being drafted to fight in Vietnam, while Lindsay's character Diane, in the movie, marries Elijah Wood's William for the same reason.

The pair talked about their roles in an interview with About.com's Rebecca Murray. Neither Lindsay nor Elijah was alive when Kennedy was murdered, so they learned a lot during filming. 'Emilio played a lot of Bobby Kennedy's speech throughout the film, and we have that there. I spoke to my grandmother, but I didn't know half of the things that I know now,' Lindsay told Murray, while Wood added: 'I also watched a lot of documentaries as well. Emilio was really forthcoming to the cast with documentary material, [including] the speech from the ballroom that night, just to familiarise [us] with the legacy of who this man was and what the event was, to really get into the mindspace of that time. It was very valuable.'

Lindsay realised it was a great way of introducing her younger fans to a part of American history. 'It was nice for me to have an opportunity to … take on the role of someone who, for my generation, for the young girl fans that I've accumulated, [they may not know about otherwise]. I actually brought my sister to the set … She didn't know who Bobby Kennedy was, and she learned so much from being there. She went home and she said stuff to her friends. It's important for me to use my celebrity status, or what it's become, in a positive way, whether it's through characters or through being with a cast of amazing people that I learned from, and just putting it out there.'

She told journalist Murray that it was cast member Sharon Stone who had influenced her the most during filming. 'She's someone that I look up to in terms of what you do for other people in the world. [She] brings a lot of awareness to that. I have more to learn from her than she does from me, in the sense that I just respect her. [She] held my hand in the scenes, and I remember grabbing [her] when I was nervous about one of the speeches I had to make. We both started to cry in the scene, and it was nice to work with someone who I didn't feel like I had to act with. I didn't feel like I had to do anything, really. It just kind of happened.'

In an interview with *Empire*, Emilio Estevez talked about when he decided to give Lindsay the role of Diane. 'Lindsay's agents kept pushing her [as a possibility for the role]. I'd heard horrible stories, so I said, "Is she interested in being thought of as a serious actress? Because this schedule can't support anybody misbehaving." They assured me, "Yes, she wants to meet with you." So I called Elijah [Wood] and said, "I need you to come to lunch today." I wanted another opinion, especially from the actor who would be in most of her scenes. It ended up as a love-fest. We laughed, we told stories, she understood the script and the role and was committed. She left, and Elijah and I looked at each other and said, "She'd be fabulous."'

He also defended her casting in a TV interview with Oprah Winfrey. 'The media focuses on allegations of her wild-child behaviour because it sells. I'd rather have them focus on how extraordinary she is in this film.'

The film itself used well-known actors to weave fictional stories around the true events that happened on the night of 5 June 1968. Robert Kennedy was, of course, the brother of the late President John F. Kennedy, who had been killed in 1963. Robert had been one of JFK's advisors in the White House, and following his brother's death he became a senator. A civil rights activist, Robert began his own campaign for the presidency of the United States in March 1968. On 5 June he won the California primary, an important landmark along the road to the presidency, and gave a rousing speech at the Ambassador Hotel in Los Angeles. Following this, he left the hotel ballroom via the kitchen, and in a crowded passageway was shot by Sirhan Sirhan. Three bullets hit Kennedy, and five other people were wounded. Robert Kennedy was rushed to hospital but died the following day.

Using newsreel footage of Kennedy, Emilio Estevez's film introduced a host of fictional characters whose business led them to the Ambassador Hotel in the hours before the assassination. There's the hotel's retired doorman (Anthony Hopkins), who spends his days playing chess with his friend (Harry Belafonte) in the lobby; an alcoholic singer (Demi Moore) and her husband (Estevez), the hotel's beautician (Sharon Stone) and her husband, the hotel manager (William H. Macy). There's Kennedy's campaign manager (Joshua Jackson) and the food manager (Christian Slater), whose racist attitude gets him fired on the day of Kennedy's arrival, plus Diane and William (Lindsay and Elijah), two young people getting married so he can avoid being sent to Vietnam.

The ensemble drama wove fact with fiction to make an interesting movie, but not one all critics agreed on. When it was released in November 2006, it received some good reviews, with BBC critic Stella Papamichael calling it 'a love letter to Robert F. Kennedy', and Angie Errigo of *Empire* writing that 'while all this threatens to tumble into soap opera with comic interludes, Estevez imaginatively summarises the 1960s zeitgeist with a persistent, aching, present-day perspective'.

There were some mixed and negative reviews, too, such as the *LA Times'* description of *Bobby* as 'an ambitious film drenched in sincerity and oozing with nostalgia that, despite the energy provided by its title icon via archival footage, falls flat dramatically in nearly every other way'. *The Village Voice* wasn't too keen either, saying that Estevez's movie 'ends up buried under its stifling good intentions and dire execution', and *Time Out*'s Dave Calhoun wrote that: '*Bobby* is hopelessly well intentioned. It's also inescapably reckless and fatally obsessed with shoehorning a celebrity into every corner.'

For Lindsay, though, it had been another movie in which she had the chance to work with some extremely talented actors, and for her to prove she was as good a performer as those older and more experienced than her. Anne Hornaday of the *Washington Post* recognised this, writing: 'In *Bobby*, that generation is most effectively embodied by a character named Diane (Lindsay Lohan), who has come to the Ambassador to marry a young man she knows only vaguely in order to keep him from going to Vietnam. Jittery and sad (her parents are boycotting the ceremony), she's also fired by the moral certainty that she's saving a life. When she explains what she's doing to a manicurist played by Sharon Stone, the unspoken wisdom between the two women is palpable and quietly electrifying.' And Moira Macdonald of the *Seattle Times* agreed: 'Lindsay Lohan is tremulous and sweet as Diane, a young woman at the hotel to marry a friend (Elijah Wood) to save him from a dangerous Vietnam assignment. In a hotel room before the quiet wedding, she unwittingly shares a secret: she's in love with him. Sharon Stone, under a blond bouffant, plays the hotel manager's beautician wife Miriam, and her scenes with Lohan (who's shyly come to the salon to get dolled up for the wedding) are surprisingly gentle.' The movie went on to be nominated for two Golden Globe Awards (Best Motion Picture, Best Original Song), and a Screen Actors Guild Award for Outstanding Performance by a Cast.

Just days after *Bobby* was released in American cinemas, Lindsay was dealt a personal blow: on 20 November Robert Altman, her supportive, caring director on *A Prairie Home Companion*, died aged eighty-one from leukaemia-related complications at Cedars-Sinai Hospital in Los Angeles. Many people spoke of their admiration for the director, while director Paul Thomas Anderson dedicated his 2007 movie *There Will Be Blood* to Altman.

Lindsay wanted to send her own condolences to Robert Altman's family, and she released a statement days after his death sending her sympathies. The letter was printed in full in newspapers, after it first appeared in the *LA Times* and began with a sincere expression of sorrow at the death of her friend: 'I would like to send my condolences out to Catherine Altman, Robert Altmans wife, as well as all of his immediate family, close friends, co-workers, and all of his inner circle.

'I feel as if I've just had the wind knocked out of me and my heart aches.

'If not only my heart but the heart of Mr Altman's wife and family and many fellow actors/artists that admire him for his work and love him for making people laugh whenever and however he could.' Lindsay went on to comment on Altman's legacy: 'The point is, he made a difference. He left us with a legend that all of us have the ability to do.' But unfortunately, as her distress rose, she became increasingly less able to express herself articulately: 'Please just take each moment day by day and consider yourself lucky to breathe and feel at all and smile. Be thankful.

'"Make a searching and fearless moral inventory of yourselves" (12st book) – everytime there's a triumph in the world a million souls hafta be trampled on – altman Its true. But treasure each triumph as they come.' and she ended with a seemingly garbled sign-off

'God Bless, peace and love always.

Thank You,

"BE ADEQUITE"

Lindsay Lohan'

Unfortunately, Lindsay's heartfelt message was criticised for its bad grammar and spelling when it was printed in the press. The *Independent*'s Andrew Gumbel commented that: 'The passion was certainly there – she, like many dozens of actors before her, clearly adored the experience of working in Altman's characteristic freeform style – but the letter was also spectacular in its incoherence and disregard of basic grammar and spelling.'

He also noted: 'The letter has become the talk of Hollywood since its release over the weekend. Was the actress on a misguided – and utterly botched – quest for publicity, exploiting the death of a revered director for her own purposes? Had she been on one of her legendary party benders? Or was this Exhibit A for the indictment of America's education system?'

Lindsay's publicist, Leslie Sloane Zelnik, issued a statement to Reuters following the criticism. 'She quickly put something together on her BlackBerry. She was devastated, she was crying . . . here was a girl who found something special in this man that she felt so close to, and she was completely shocked and blown away that he had just died. It was written very quickly, and it was from the heart.'

To anyone on the outside, it was obvious that things were not going well for Lindsay and that she needed help. She was saddened by Altman's death, distressed by her father's imprisonment and her parents' continuing divorce proceedings, and by forever being followed by the paparazzi and criticised for her lifestyle. As 2006 ended, something had to give, and on 3 December 2006, it was revealed that Lindsay was seeking some help of her own, by going to Alcoholics Anonymous meetings.

The *New York Post* reported days before that Lindsay had been seen going to AA, and Leslie Sloane Zelnik confirmed the reports, saying: 'She started attending some, and it is a positive thing. It's a place to go and feel safe. No one judges her, and it's going to be a slow process. But to me, the fact that she's seeing that there's something not right makes her smarter than the next person.' Sloane also spoke to *People*, asking for some privacy for Lindsay. 'Yes, she's been attending some meetings, and it's going to be a slow process. This is a positive. Let's hope that the press doesn't turn it into a negative. Maybe if [the press] backs off, she'll be in a good space. Let's see if we don't have to hear about it every day, and they're following her and trying to find her. Because that will just not be good.'

Lindsay's mother Dina was also asked about Lindsay's AA meetings when she was interviewed by Ryan Seacrest on Los Angeles radio station KIIS FM. 'It's true. A lot of people she hangs out with go, and it's a positive thing.' Seacrest also asked Dina if she gave Lindsay advice about her Hollywood lifestyle. 'As a parent, you tell them what you can tell them, but she's twenty and I'm not gonna say, stay home and don't go out. That's a ridiculous thing to do. When you're twenty you have to learn a lot on your own, so I'm there for support and I'll obviously give her my opinion, but she's fine. She's OK.'

Perhaps Lindsay was hoping for a new start as a difficult 2006 came to an end, but as 2007 began, things didn't look any easier for her. On 3 January 2007, while working on a new movie called *I Know Who Killed Me*, Lindsay was diagnosed with appendicitis and admitted to hospital to have her appendix removed. Dina emailed the TV show *Access Hollywood* the following day to say that Lindsay was back at home following the operation on Friday 5 January. 'Lindsay is recovering quickly and is eager to get back to work. The doctors and nurses are extremely happy with her quick recovery. Thank you for your prayers and support.'

She returned to the set of *I Know Who Killed Me* soon after, but less than two weeks after her appendectomy, Lindsay's health made headlines again.

On Wednesday 17 January, she released a statement to the press as it was revealed she had checked into a rehab facility. 'I have made a proactive decision to take care of my personal health,' she said. 'I appreciate your well wishes and ask that you please respect my privacy at this time.'

Us Weekly reported that Lindsay had entered the Wonderland Center in Los Angeles' Laurel Canyon at 2.30 p.m. that day. *Us Weekly*'s celebrity reporter Noelle Hancock wrote: 'She arrived at the facility in a blacked-out SUV followed by a caravan of two other cars.

Looking sombre, the actress carried a dark Balenciaga bag and a Jamba Juice, she wore black tights, a green flannel shirt, a leather jacket and a black baseball cap that said 'Lola'.

The Wonderland Center is an alcohol and drug rehabilitation and treatment centre with Howard Samuels as its executive director. A recovering cocaine and heroin addict who has been sober for over twenty-five years, Samuels was interviewed by the *Guardian* newspaper in 2009 about his beliefs with regard to addiction. 'It really is about the willingness of the client,' he said. 'That's going to be the key to long-term success. I'm not a believer that treatment centres save people's lives. If you've got a really good treatment centre, you can go a long way towards helping a person, but at the end of the day it's not about the treatment centre. It's about the individual, and about whether or not they're at that place to change.'

Unlike many other treatment facilities, Wonderland allows short stays of a week to 30 days and, according to the *Guardian*, residents are allowed to use their mobile phones and computers and carry on their business during the day. This meant that Lindsay could continue filming her new movie, as long as she returned to rehab every night. The centre has been criticised for this unusual way of operating, with John MacDougall of the Hazelden centre commenting for the *Guardian* article on how different his facility was to Wonderland: 'No one leaves here – except for a funeral, if a close relative dies. We ask you to commit for twenty-eight days. Actually, I can only remember one exception in the fourteen years I've been here, and he had to present a treaty at the United Nations.'

Reporter Amanda Fortini wrote the following description of Wonderland: 'The Wonderland Center occupies a $7m property on Mulholland Drive. Behind a massive iron gate, three cream-coloured houses with terracotta roofs are set back from the road by a long, winding path that staff members navigate with golf buggies. The bedrooms are simple, with crisp white duvet covers and wooden armoires. (There are only six single rooms, because clients often have, in the parlance of Wonderland, 'a tendency to isolate'.) There are two small kidney bean-shaped pools and two sprawling patios. Here, between sessions, clients lounge on wrought-iron furniture and talk and text and smoke. One has the overwhelming sense of attending a weekend party at a cosy but understated house.'

During her time at Wonderland, Lindsay missed the Sundance Film Festival, where another movie she had made the previous year, *Chapter 27*, was shown to the press for the first time. Like *Bobby*, it was based on a real event – the shooting of John Lennon by Mark David Chapman.

John Lennon, of course, found fame as one of The Beatles, one of the most popular bands in music history. Born in Liverpool in 1940, Lennon first formed a band called The Quarrymen when he was a teenager, and this eventually evolved into the famous Beatles line up of Lennon, Paul McCartney, George Harrison and Ringo Starr. By 1963, the Fab Four, as they became known, were huge stars in Britain and by 1965 they were known around the world for songs such as 'Twist And Shout', 'Can't Buy Me Love' and 'Help!'. By 1970, The Beatles was no more, but John also recorded as a solo artist with his girlfriend, and then wife, Yoko Ono, writing and recording songs such as the classics 'Mother', 'Imagine' and 'Happy Xmas (War Is Over)'.

Lennon and Ono moved to New York in 1971 and they both became known for their anti-war stance with regard to the Vietnam War. By 1975, it seemed John had retired from music and was happy to spend time with his family, including his newborn son with Yoko, Sean Lennon (he also had an older son, Julian, with first wife Cynthia). In 1980, however, John released his first single in five years, '(Just Like) Starting Over', followed by the album *Double Fantasy* in November 1980.

On 8 December 1980, just before 11 p.m., John Lennon and Yoko Ono were returning to their apartment at the Dakota Building on New York's Upper West Side after an evening out when Mark David Chapman – who had asked Lennon to sign his copy of *Double Fantasy* earlier that day – shot John in the back four times. John Lennon was pronounced dead at the nearby Roosevelt Hospital at 11.07 p.m.

Making a movie about the man who had murdered John Lennon was controversial, especially as many of the people depicted in the film - including Chapman - are still alive. Sean Lennon, who was five when his father was killed, told the TV news programme *The Insider* that he believed the film was 'tacky'.

The movie was written and directed by J. P. Schaefer, a film graduate making his directorial debut. Unlike a film made the previous year, *The Killing of John Lennon*, which focused on three months in Chapman's life before the shooting, *Chapter 27* centred on just three days, 6 to 9 December 1980. Jared Leto, best known for his role in the series *My So-Called Life*, starred as Chapman. The actor gained a reported 50lbs for the role, telling Starpulse.com how he did it. 'I was eating everything you think you're not supposed to - pizza, pasta, ice cream, but my little trick was I would take pints of chocolate Häagen-Dazs and put them in the microwave and drink them. The sick thing is I would actually pour olive oil and soy sauce into the mixture as well - to get me bloated even more.' The weight gain was so extreme he ended up in a wheelchair, as Leto told Boston.com. 'My body was in shock from the amount of weight I gained. I don't know if it was gout, but I had a definite problem with my feet. I couldn't walk for long distances. I had a wheelchair because it was so painful.'

'It was important to make that transformation. It changed everything about who I was - the way I walked, talked, how I felt about myself and the way people treated me. It was interesting to see what people thought – some obviously thought I'd let myself go. I'd never do it again, it definitely gave me some problems. It took about a year to feel semi-normal. I don't know if I'll ever be back to the place I was physically.'

In an interview with Paul Fischer during filming of the movie in 2006, Lindsay spoke about her role in the movie as a Lennon fan Chapman meets, and what attracted her to a role in a film about John Lennon's murder. 'I sat down with Yoko Ono a few times to talk to her about it . . . it's a very touchy subject, and nobody wanted me to do the movie, that worked for me [talking to Yoko]. Just because John Lennon is a legend. I was actually really nervous going into it, because I did get death threats, but the director I believe in, and he's a good friend of mine.'

She added: 'I love my character in the movie, she's just such a genuine fan of John Lennon and Yoko Ono. She's the light in the movie – she's like the Hitchcock blonde, but I'm not blond in it. But she reminds me of that. Jarrett Schaeffer's a great director, and he's doing a great job with it, and Jared Leto did a great job. It was interesting to me. But I wanted to get the OK from Yoko Ono.'

Following the film's debut at the Sundance Film Festival, it struggled to find a distributor to place the film in US cinemas and wasn't released to the public until March 2008, where it was shown on just a handful of screens before disappearing onto DVD. At Sundance, it had also got a mixed reception. Salon.com said that Lindsay was 'pretty good – a ray of light in the rapidly darkening gloom of his [Chapman's] world', but most reviews had more in common with Jim Emerson's in the *Chicago Sun-Times*, which said: '*Chapter 27* just makes you feel bad for, and about, everybody – including the wretched souls who made the thing.'

As Lindsay emerged from her stay at the Wonderland rehab facility, she must have wanted to put *Chapter 27*, and the events of the previous year, behind her. She had been at Wonderland for thirty days, and returned home on 19 February 2007. 'Lindsay has finished her stay at Wonderland and will continue the programme as an outpatient,' her publicist Leslie Sloane Zelnik said in a statement. She is taking it one day at a time, as she is in it for the long haul. She asks that her privacy be respected.'

Of course, *that* was never going to happen . . .

Chapter Eight
I Know Who Killed Me

2007 had not started well for Lindsay. While in rehab at the Wonderland Center, she had been working on her next movie, *I Know Who Killed Me*, but had pulled out of the project she was scheduled to work on after that. Her publicist, Leslie Sloane Zelnik, had told *People* on 1 February that Lindsay would no longer be making the movie *A Woman of No Importance*, based on the Oscar Wilde play of the same name, which was also to star Annette Bening.

'She doesn't just want to say yes to everyone and compromise herself any more,' Sloane Zelnik said of Lindsay's decision not to do the movie. 'If anything has been learned, it's that what she needs comes first –

and right now she needs focus. It's a mature thing to do … She's doing this so she can focus on getting better.' Sloane added: 'Lindsay is sad that she's unable finally to get to work with Annette, because she's a huge fan and respects her.' (In the end, the movie was not made at all.)

Meanwhile, Lindsay's mother Dina had given an interview to *Harper's Bazaar* while Lindsay was in rehab, talking about her daughter's problems. Interviewer Phoebe Easton asked Dina whether she thought it had been a good idea to encourage Lindsay to go out partying by going with her. 'Listen to me: Lindsay would drag me, literally drag my loser butt [to parties] and say, "I need you to know who these people are." Yeah, she trusts my judgement. She's in such a whirlwind; she's in a tornado.

'Lindsay had to fall and get up,' Dina added, talking about her rehab. 'I knew it was coming. I told her, but finally she was like, "Mommy, I had to do it myself." You can lead a horse to water. You can't make him drink.'

The *Harper's Bazaar* article went on to mention that gossip columns had dubbed Dina the 'momager' because, as well as being Lindsay's mother, she remained one of her daughter's business managers. 'We're just so misunderstood,' Dina said about her family. 'My sons are in sports, my daughters want to be actors. I was in the business, and I'm going to help them. You don't like that? I'm living the American dream, and you can go ***'

Still, not everyone thought Dina working with Lindsay was helping her daughter. The *New York Post*'s entertainment reporters wrote that Dina had visited Lindsay in Wonderland . . . and brought an *Entertainment Tonight* film crew with her. A nameless source commented: 'Dina wants to be a TV star.'

A *Vanity Fair* article entitled 'Moms Gone Wild' mentioned Dina alongside other mothers with daughters in the public eye, including Kathy Hilton (mum of Paris) and Lynne Spears (mother of Britney). In the article, Dina was interviewed about the drink problems that had taken Lindsay to the Wonderland Center. 'Lindsay's no different than any other twenty-year-old girl who's doing some experimenting,' she told Judith Newman. 'It's just that when we did this kind of thing we didn't have cameras turned on us all the time. What were you doing when you were twenty, for goodness' sake?'

In the same article, *Us Weekly* editor Janice Min speculated that Dina sometimes overlooked Lindsay's problems. 'When Lindsay lost a dramatic amount of weight two years ago, Dina Lohan called to arrange a meeting with me,' Min told *Vanity Fair*. 'She was very nice, very protective of Lindsay, but very willing to look beyond what seemed like obvious problems with food. "These things happen – she's a girl who lost her baby fat." She has blind spots. In the end she might not be helping her daughter by not giving her a sense of accountability.'

An unnamed network executive who met Dina – now occasionally working as a red-carpet reporter for *Entertainment Tonight* – when she was pitching a reality show about the Lohan family, also commented to *Vanity Fair* that Dina was 'warm and sincere, but totally deluded. [In Dina's head] Lindsay's this totally normal kid, a girl like anyone else, who just has the normal problems of youth. Only because of the fact that she's in entertainment does she find it hard to make friends and trust people – as if that explains it.

'My feeling about her,' the executive continued, 'is not so much that she craves fame. I think it's money. I think she is very angry. She's had a tough time in her marriage, and for quite a while Lindsay has been pretty much the sole support of her family.'

Us Weekly's Janice Min added: 'People on staff here have seen Dina out partying with her daughter. But look, she's a woman who spent her twenties and thirties raising children in a terrible marriage. In the way that Lindsay and Britney were these child stars who are having a delayed adolescence, she's having a delayed adolescence. Or worse than that: a delayed youth. That stress of scraping by, keeping your family intact when your husband is a ne'er-do-well . . . Dina is doing what a lot of women in that situation do, which is holding it together as best she can.'

As Lindsay emerged from the Wonderland Center on 19 February, she knew all eyes were on her following the *Vanity Fair* article (and many others). Just five days later, on 24 February, the 27th Golden Raspberry Awards (aka the Razzies, awarded for the worst films and performances of the year) were announced, with Lindsay unfortunately in the running for Worst Actress for her performance in *Just My Luck*. It was one award she was probably glad not to win – instead, Lindsay's *Bobby* co-star Sharon Stone took home the prize for her performance in *Basic Instinct 2*. Luckily, the Razzies aren't taken too seriously, with everyone from Halle Berry (who collected her award in person – usually recipients stay away from the ceremony) to Sandra Bullock, Laurence Olivier, Kevin Costner and Bruce Willis having received an award in the course of their careers.

While Lindsay had to watch out for the prying cameras of the paparazzi that were waiting to catch her reaction to such news, or catch her out at parties and celebrity functions, there were two photo shoots she was looking forward to being made public. Before staying at Wonderland, Lindsay had done a sexy photo shoot for *GQ* that appeared on their April issue cover in March 2007, with a brief interview that she had done via her Blackberry while in rehab. She had also signed up as the face of Miu Miu – Prada's younger fashion line – at the end of 2006, and her first modelling photographs for the spring/summer 2007 campaign were a huge hit when they were published: Lindsay, with flame-red hair and dramatic make-up, looked absolutely stunning. Both sets of photographs, for *GQ* and

Miu Miu, were met with praise, with fashion blog PurseBlog.com describing the Miu Miu pictures as 'elegant, sleek and sophisticated'.

For the first time in a while, things were looking more positive for Lindsay. She also received news that her father, Michael Lohan, was due for release from prison on 13 March, having served more than two years in jail. It was also reported by news website anorak.co.uk that he was a different man from the one who had been imprisoned at Collins Correctional Center. Brett Hudson, who was planning to produce a reality show called *Hollywood Dad* with Lohan, told the press: 'Michael Lohan is a changed man. I've spoken to him often, and I know it. The last time around, Michael would never admit he'd done anything wrong. Now, he not only admits his past mistakes, but he wants to right the wrongs he's done. And most of all, he wants to get his family back on track.'

Anorak.co.uk also reported that Michael had been ordained as a minister while in jail. 'He's serious about it. He's actually going straight into the ministry when he gets out - the Teen Challenge Ministry to help runaways and kids on drugs, trying to straighten out their lives,' Hudson confirmed. 'He's still Michael in more than one way,' he added. 'He's still very creative. You can see where Lindsay got her drive and her talent. He has a few reality shows he wants to pitch - including one in which he and Lindsay are put on a desert island with Paris Hilton, Jessica Simpson and their dads.

We'll be going along when he does that. We'll be with him when he tries to "save" some of his old Hollywood pals. And he's got other ideas, like going out on Sunset Boulevard and giving a prostitute a hundred-dollar bill – not for sex, but for her time so he can talk to her and try and save her. He wants to make things right with the world. And especially his family.'

Michael became a resident of a Teen Challenge centre in West Babylon, Long Island, following his release from prison. It was there that he gave an interview to Spencer Morgan of the *New York Observer*, talking about how he had changed. 'It's the same thing as in Luke 9 verse 24,' Lohan told Morgan. 'If you want to be saved – if a man wants to save his life, a man has to lose his life. And basically, that's what happened to me, I lost my life when I hit that pole [the 2005 car accident that led to his arrest], and I found a new life.'

Lohan spoke about how everything changed for the better for him. 'I'm in Nassau County Jail, I'm walking in the dorm … so I come back to my bunk and there's a number on my bunk and it says "Teen Challenge" on it. I look at it and I'm like, "What's this Teen Challenge thing?" I called the number and found out it was a faith-based rehabilitation programme.' Michael went on to describe the day in prison when he was reborn. 'I was in the middle of the dorm, and everyone is looking at Michael Lohan, on his knees, crying, and I accepted the Lord. From that point on, Teen Challenge became the focus of my life.'

He also spoke about how he wanted to help Lindsay in the interview. "'Can you imagine" - my pastor, Jimmy, keeps telling me this - "Mike, can you imagine if Lindsay or Paris Hilton or Nicole Richie, or all of them, or one of them - especially Lindsay - turned it all around? Lindsay's example could be the greatest sermon to millions of people across the world. A story of redemption, a real Cinderella story.'" However, he admitted he had had little contact with his daughter since his release, though he was hoping that would change. 'If I did tell you [what I have spoken about with Lindsay], it would ruin any future contact with my daughter,' he told Morgan. 'My contact and communication with Lindsay, I don't find it necessary to make public.'

He did, however, talk about how hard it was to watch the trials and tribulations in Lindsay's life from afar. 'All these people who don't know what she is going through are trying to help her. It's hard to help someone get through something, unless you have been through it yourself ... You know what hurt the most? I wanted to be there for her, and everyone who caused the division in our family kept me away; *they* were afraid that, because I've come back to be the person the Lord wants me to be and that everyone loves, that if I become a part of Lindsay's life and it turns around, everybody is going to say, "She just needed a father all along."'

If newspaper reports were to be believed, Lindsay

certainly needed someone to help her – the tabloids were noting that she was back partying on a regular basis, with the *New York Daily News* commenting that on 20 March she was seen at New York's Unik club being approached by former boyfriend Wilmer Valderrama. A clubber told the newspaper that Wilmer 'tried to talk to her, but she didn't have much time for him. Then he grabbed a microphone and said, "Lindsay, this is for you."'

Wilmer reportedly went on to sing Matchbox 20's 'Back 2 Good', a song about a romantic relationship gone wrong. According to the *New York Daily News*'s source, Lindsay shouted, 'It's too late,' to Wilmer, who left a few minutes later.

The press were quick to speculate who Lindsay might be dating, if it wasn't Wilmer, and in May it was revealed that the new man in her life was Calum Best. Five years older than Lindsay, Calum was best known in Britain as the son of legendary footballer George Best and ex-Playboy bunny Angela Janes.

Born in San Jose, California in 1981, Calum was mainly raised in the US, where his mother returned after her marriage to Best broke down in 1986. Being the son of George Best – considered one of the best footballers in the world, and also known as a notorious hell-raiser and alcoholic – made Calum well known in the UK. He began his career as a fashion model before appearing in a series of reality shows including *The Match*, and a eyebrow-raising show called *Celebrity Love*

Island. The idea behind the show was that twelve celebrities were flown to an island in Fiji, with the idea that they might find romance with someone else on the island. Viewers could vote a couple into the 'love shack', where the pair got some alone time; they also voted to send someone home each episode. Calum appeared in both seasons of *Celebrity Love Island*, and won the second series.

Appearing in the show cemented his image as something of a ladies' man, like his father, and by the time he began dating Lindsay he was known for his prowess with women, with Kate Moss, model Agyness Dean and actress Gemma Atkinson reputed to be among his exes. Soon Calum and Lindsay's relationship was all over the gossip columns. *People* reported seeing them at the opening of the Cove at Atlantis Paradise Island resort in the Bahamas on 14 May, with the magazine's reporter Steve Helling writing that 'the pair moved on to the after-party at the Aura nightclub, where they shared several kisses in a VIP booth. On Saturday, the couple spent several hours in a private cabana on Cove Beach. As the temperatures soared, Best rubbed sunblock on Lohan's shoulders before they headed into the water for swimming, splashing and still more kissing. That evening, they returned to Aura, where they sat in the same booth as they had the night before. 'They seem to have had a wonderful weekend,' says an onlooker. 'They're enjoying their time in paradise.'

Unfortunately for Lindsay, Calum was allegedly

soon chatting about their relationship, with *The People* newspaper interviewing a 'source' who said: 'He told me "She's dynamite between the sheets ... No girl I've ever slept with comes close".'

The source went on to say: 'Calum was knocked out by her body. He said she's got one of the best he's ever seen, with all the curves in the right places.' Not surprisingly, Lindsay and Calum's steamy relationship had soon burned out, although they did see each other on and off over the next year. It seemed for the best – Calum was caught out just weeks later by the *Sun* newspaper, who videoed him 'enjoying a three-hour orgy with two hookers and copious lines of cocaine', while the following year a sex tape emerged, made on a mobile phone, that had people wondering whether it was him and Lindsay in 2007, or, more likely, a fake. It was more bad publicity that she didn't need.

Unfortunately, there was more to come. Lindsay had had to pull out of one upcoming movie, *The Edge of Love*, in which she was due to play the wife of Dylan Thomas, because Lindsay was unable to film in Wales 'for insurance reasons', as the director John Maybury told BBC News (the film went ahead with Sienna Miller taking Lindsay's role, alongside Keira Knightley and Matthew Rhys). Then she was due to start shooting a movie called *Poor Things*, described as a 'grandma gang' comedy, with Shirley MacLaine and Olympia Dukakis, but just days before the production was due to start, Lindsay was arrested. It was 26 May, and, as CNN News reported: 'Beverly Hills police arrested actress Lindsay Lohan on Saturday for driving under the influence of alcohol, a police spokesman said. Lohan, 20, lost control of her 2005 Mercedes-Benz convertible and struck a kerb early Saturday morning, Lt Mitch McCann told reporters. She received treatment for minor injuries at Century City Doctors hospital, where police cited and arrested her. Because of her injuries, police released Lohan on the misdemeanour charge, McCann said. McCann also said police found "additional contraband" in Lohan's car, which has been preliminarily identified as a "usable" amount of cocaine.'

Three days later, it was reported that Lindsay was returning to rehab following her arrest. Her publicist, Leslie Sloane Zelnik, told CBS News in a statement that Lindsay 'admitted herself to an intensive medical rehabilitation facility. Because this is a medical matter, it is our hope that the press will appreciate the seriousness of the situation and respect the privacy of Lindsay as well as the other patients receiving treatment at the facility.'

The producers of *Poor Things*, Rob Hickman and Shirley MacLaine, released a statement following Lindsay's arrest. 'In the spirit of helping Lindsay Lohan and her rehabilitation, we have been asked by Lindsay to comply with her wishes to continue working on *Poor Things*. We are trying to rearrange the shooting schedule to facilitate her working at the end of the shoot, to coincide with the completion of her rehabilitation. We wish her love and the blending of mind, body and spirit.'

Lindsay was scheduled to appear in court in August with regard to the crash, and in the meantime she checked into Promises for forty-five days. This treatment centre was different from the Wonderland facility where Lindsay had stayed at the beginning of the year in that Promises patients cannot come and go so easily, and they are encouraged to stay for at least one month. There are two Promises centres, one in Malibu (where Lindsay stayed) and one in West Los Angeles, and both provide treatment for addiction to drugs and alcohol. In July 2007, the *New York Times* reported that a stay at Promises cost $49,000 a month, while the Promises website states that it is 'designed for clients who are accustomed to luxury, including celebrities, business executives, government officials and others who prefer superior-quality addiction treatment in a beautiful setting and where the highest privacy standards are required.' Britney Spears and Matthew Perry are among the celebrities who have been treated there.

Lindsay emerged from rehab on 15 July, wearing a SCRAM bracelet – a Secure Continuous Remote Alcohol Monitoring device – which estimates the blood alcohol content of the body by measuring the ethanol content of perspiration. The idea was to keep her on the straight and narrow by keeping her away from alcohol, but just ten days later it was announced by Los Angeles police that Lindsay had been arrested again, on suspicion of drink-driving and possession of cocaine.

Lt Alex Padilla told reporters that Lindsay was arrested near Santa Monica police station, after the mother of one of Lindsay's assistants reported a car chase. Lindsay was allegedly chasing her, she said, after the assistant had quit her job hours before. 'Why she was trying to catch her, we don't know,' said Padilla. 'The mother tried to make it here to the Santa Monica Police Department. She didn't make it here. She ended up in the parking lot, and that's when she called the police department on her cell phone and we responded. The mother was afraid. She wasn't quite sure what was going on, so she called the police because she wanted to make sure everything would be OK.'

Reporters for the *Los Angeles Times* noted that 'authorities found Lohan and the other driver in a "heated debate" in the parking lot of Santa Monica's Civic Auditorium about 1.30 a.m. Lohan refused a sobriety test at the scene but was tested at the station, Padilla said. The test found her blood alcohol between .12 and .13 per cent, he said. California's legal limit is .08 percent. Padilla said that while Lohan was at the station, officers discovered a small amount of cocaine in her pocket. The actress was booked on two misde-meanour charges of driving under the influence of alcohol and driving on a suspended licence, and a felony charge of possession of cocaine, police said.'

Lindsay's lawyer, Blair Berk, issued a statement following the arrest. 'Addiction is a terrible and vicious disease. Since Lindsay's transition to outpatient care, she has been monitored on a SCRAM bracelet and tested daily in order to support her sobriety. Throughout this period, I have received timely and accurate reports from the testing company. Unfortunately, late yesterday I was informed that Lindsay had relapsed. The bracelet has now been removed. She is safe, out of custody and presently receiving medical care.'

She was released the following morning after paying $25,000 in bail. At the same time, dad Michael released a statement to the press saying he and his wife should place aside their own 'legal battle for the good of our children. When we were a family, did you see any of this going on? It wasn't until we were torn apart, at the pinnacle of Lindsay's career, no less, when people came into the picture, did everything fall apart,' he told *Access Hollywood*. 'The walls that have been put between us is what's causing this to happen.'

Just days after her arrest, Lindsay's most recent movie, *I Know Who Killed Me*, was released in cinemas in the US. But as David Halbfinger of the *New York Times* commented, it wasn't perhaps the best time for her to have a new movie out. Lindsay had been due to promote the movie on the high-profile chat show *The Tonight Show*, but following her arrest her appearance was cancelled. Production on her upcoming movie *Poor Things* had been halted, and Halbfinger interviewed a Hollywood insider Bernie Brillstein (whose company had represented John Belushi before his death) to see what effect Lindsay's arrest would have on her career. 'I hope they put her in jail for as long as they can. Maybe she'll realise how serious it is. I believe she's uninsurable. And when you're uninsurable in this town, you're done.'

I Know Who Killed Me was released with little fanfare – Tristar Pictures didn't even allow the press to see it before it was released (usually, critics are invited to see a movie weeks in advance so they can review it). The movie was an adult thriller, with Lindsay in the lead role of Aubrey Fleming. A serial killer is stalking the town of New Salem, one who abducts and tortures young women, holding them captive for weeks before killing them. Aubrey disappears after a night out with friends and the FBI are desperate to find her before it is too late.

One night, Aubrey is found by the side of the road, critically injured. In hospital, her parents (Julia Ormond and Neal McDonough) are by her bedside as she slips in and out of consciousness, but when she comes round she says she isn't Aubrey, her name is Dakota Moss and she's a stripper. The doctors think Aubrey is suffering from post-traumatic stress disorder, but even when she returns home with her parents she insists she is Dakota, not Aubrey. Could Aubrey and

Dakota be twins? And if that is true, does that mean Aubrey is still being held by the serial killer?

While the movie's plot sounds interesting, critics didn't agree, and there were some bad reviews. *The Hollywood Reporter* said it was 'a fresh candidate in the running for worst movie of 2007 honours', while Jeanette Catsoulis of the *New York Times* wrote that 'pretentious and inane, *I Know Who Killed Me* arouses unexpected sympathy for its embattled star'. TV critic Richard Roeper named it his number-one worst movie of the noughties and the film went on to be nominated for nine Razzies, for which it won eight in 2008, including Worst Actress (for Lindsay), Worst Director, Worst Screenplay and even a new category, Worst Excuse For A Horror Movie.

There were some slightly more positive reviews with horror magazine *Fangoria* favourably comparing it to Dario Argento's horror classic *Suspiria*, and Britain's *Radio Times* calling it a 'twisty, perversely fascinating psycho thriller'. The film's screenwriter, Jeff Hammond, talked about the film in an interview with the horror website Bloody Disgusting!. 'My first reaction [to Lindsay's casting] was … wow! My little horror film suddenly wasn't so little any more. I still don't think I've fully absorbed the meaning of having someone this big in our movie. Lindsay Lohan has a great natural talent. I can't imagine any other actress breathing as much life into the characters of Aubrey and Dakota. I couldn't be happier with her performance.'

Unfortunately, the movie did badly at the box office, making only $9.7 million in the US. It seemed people were currently more interested in Lindsay's private life than seeing her on screen, but she sensibly took a step back from the headlines and the limelight. She admitted herself to the Cirque Lodge rehabilitation programme in Utah, where she went bike-riding and white-water rafting during her stay. The centre, whose celebrity clients have included Melanie Griffith, Kirsten Dunst, David Hasselhoff and Eva Mendes, was more private and rural than the rehab facilities Lindsay had visited before. *Fortune* magazine's Claudia Wallis got a rare glimpse inside Cirque Lodge, and wrote that 'even before you set foot inside the Cirque Lodge, it's monumentally obvious why people would come here. The Lodge – a stunning structure of fieldstone, glass, and wood – sits just up the mountain from Utah's Sundance Resort, a stone's throw from Robert Redford's Rocky Mountains estate. With rooms for just sixteen residents, it commands views that could literally lift you up when you've hit bottom.' The centre follows the twelve-step Alcoholics Anonymous programme, offering patients therapy, support meetings, exercise and meditation during their stays.

On 23 August, it was quietly announced that Lindsay's lawyers had negotiated a plea deal on her driving cases, meaning she would not have to go to court. Lindsay pleaded guilty to two counts of being under the influence of cocaine, and pleaded no contest to the charge of reckless driving. She was originally sentenced to four days in jail, reduced to forty-eight hours to take into account the time she had spent in police custody when she was arrested, but it was agreed that this could be amended to one day and ten days community service; she was also sentenced to three years probation, and ordered to complete an eighteen-month alcohol education programme.

'Lohan received the same sentence that anyone else with a second DUI conviction would get. She got no special treatment,' said Deputy District Attorney Danette Meyers in a statement. Lindsay released a statement shortly after her sentencing.

'It is clear to me that my life has become completely unmanageable because I am addicted to alcohol and drugs. Recently, I relapsed and did things for which I am ashamed. I broke the law, and today I took responsibility by pleading guilty to the charges in my case. No matter what I said when I was under the influence on the day I was arrested, I am not blaming anyone else for my conduct other than myself. I thank God I did not injure others. I easily could have.

'I very much want to be healthy and gain control of my life and career, and have asked for medical help in doing so. I am taking these steps to improve my life. Luckily, I am not alone in my daily struggle, and I know that people like me have succeeded. Maybe with time it will become easier. I hope so.'

Lindsay remained at Cirque Lodge until 5 October.

A source told *People* in a statement that: 'she's finished the programme. Lindsay is done, but she may come back for outpatient treatment. She overextended her stay because she wanted to. She could have been out a while ago, but she chose to stay.'

Lindsay's parents both spoke to the press about her recovery. 'I'm proud of her,' mother Dina told *People*. 'She's moving ahead with her life. Things were getting out of control. She took action. She took responsibility. She really needed to heal.' Meanwhile, it was father Michael who collected Lindsay from the Utah centre, telling the magazine: 'I will be there in her life as best I can, but from here on she's going to have a lot of decisions to make on her own. Now that she is going out into the world, I can only hope for the best.' It seemed that Lindsay and her father had reunited while she was in rehab, speaking for the first time in three years. 'I'm enjoying my time with Lindsay, and I'm happy to see and believe she's the Lindsay I last saw three years ago, before all this turmoil came into her life,' Michael told *People*. 'I am trying my best to lead by example and institute important tools.'

Dina seemed to approve, adding that the reunion between father and daughter 'can only help her recovery. It's time to mend.' Indeed, while Lindsay had been in rehab, Michael and Dina had finally resolved their differences, finalising their divorce in mid-August without involving a messy court case that would have revealed what had gone on behind closed doors in their marriage. On 13 August, Michael told the press: 'Dina and I are working everything out, and we will have an agreement signed by next Friday. I hope to be reunited with my children very shortly and be part of their lives.'

It seemed, for now at least, that all was well with Lindsay's family. Lindsay had even met a new boyfriend, Riley Giles, while she was at Cirque Lodge, about whom her father told *People*: 'He's a great, great kid. If you met him, you'd like him.' Once the relationship ended two months later in November, however, ungallant snow-boarder Giles sold his story for a reported $200,000 to the British tabloid *News of the World*, describing his ex-girlfriend as a sex maniac. 'Lindsay's definitely a nymphomaniac. She's wild in bed. We'd have sex a couple of times in the day and then go to it through the night,' he told the paper. 'We once did it four times in a row straight. That was crazy. Lindsay was insatiable. She'd demand sex again and again. We'd go at it for hours. She'd have worn out most guys.'

He continued: 'The first time we had sex I couldn't believe I was looking down at Lindsay Lohan naked. We'd barely gotten through the door when we just ripped each other's clothes off. Lindsay is so hot. She has a great body. Her backside is fantastic, perfect, all plump and round.'

He went on to explain their break-up. 'She's a great person, but it's hard to have a girlfriend who's sur-rounded by movie stars and doing whatever she wants.

Sure, her friends were all nice. But anyone can put on a face, and I don't know how sincere they were. There are a lot of fakes in LA.' (And quite a few kiss-and-tell merchants, it seems.)

While Lindsay did not comment on his kiss-and-tell story, her mother did. 'He took desperate measures to hurt Lindsay because she broke up with him,' Dina told *People*.

Sensibly, Lindsay took all this in her stride and set about returning to work. Before she could start, however, there was the matter of her jail sentence for the drunk-driving offences.

On 15 November, Lindsay turned herself in to the Los Angeles County Women's Detention Center in Lynwood at 10.30 a.m. According to the Associated Press, she was searched, fingerprinted and placed in a holding cell but remained in her clothes rather than wearing prison uniform. 'She was cooperative,' said sheriff's spokesman Steve Whitmore. Then, just eighty-four minutes later, at 11.54 a.m, Lindsay was released. Her day sentence had been reduced, taking into account the fact that the prison was overcrowded and her crime non-violent. (According to the Associated Press, between thirty and fifty women are granted early release from Lynwood every day.)

She wasn't the first young female celebrity to spend time in jail in 2007. Two of her friends had also spent time in prison – Paris Hilton and Nicole Richie. Paris had served twenty-three days at Lynwood following a series of driving offences earlier that year. Nicole Richie, meanwhile, had had an even shorter sentence than Lindsay. Arrested in December 2006 after witnesses reported her car going the wrong way down a freeway in Burbank, California, she pleaded guilty to a drink-driving charge in July 2007 and spent just eighty-two minutes in custody.

Now Lindsay was home again, it was time to get back to work. However, much of Hollywood was worried that she would relapse again, and her health was also a concern to insurance companies. Actors are always insured when they work on a movie (for accidents, unexpected illness and other circumstances that could cause a delay in production), and if no insurance company would take a chance on Lindsay, she wouldn't be able to work.

Hollywood publicist Michael Levine predicted in an interview with ABC News that Lindsay would not be employable for a while. 'For the next eighteen months, no way. No deal. This makes Paris Hilton's problems look minimal,' he said. 'She's got to get herself in the hands of some very serious rehabilitation specialists for a long period of time. If she's able to make a statement where she accepts responsibility and does whatever it takes to get well, that would be preferable.'

An unnamed Los Angeles talent agent also spoke to ABC about Lindsay's current problems. 'Say you're going to make a $5 million movie, and you're hiring

Lindsay Lohan as the lead. Right away, you have insurance should she fall, break a leg or get injured. But to know that she has this history – what insurance company is going to want to hop on board? What if she doesn't come to work for three days, and you have to pay $300,000 to keep the set going?'

Producers of *Poor Things* had already made the decision to move on with production of the movie without Lindsay. One insurer suggested how Lindsay should proceed. 'Generally speaking, for actors with insurability problems ... what we'll do is structure a programme where there's a very big carrot for doing the right thing,' said Brian Kingman, a broker who specialised in insuring films. 'The actor's got to defer their salary; they'll only get paid if they complete, so that's their incentive. Of course some of them get paid a lot already, so that doesn't really matter.'

'Film-makers put up millions and millions of dollars on a movie, studios put up hundreds of millions of dollars, and it requires everybody's professionalism,' Kingman added. 'When somebody isn't professional, that gives insurers concerns. Whether its health or lifestyle issues, those need to be addressed.'

As 2007 drew to a close, it looked like there was a tough road ahead for Lindsay if she wanted to get her career back on track. But she could draw comfort from the fact that, as publicist Michael Levine told ABC, if there is one thing the public loves, it is a comeback. 'I think Robert Downey Jr might well be an example of that. In the long term, anything's possible.'

Downey Jr is, of course, a great example of someone who turned his life and career around. A child actor who had made his name as an adult in movies such as *Less Than Zero*, *Chaplin* (for which he received a Best Actor Academy Award nomination) and *Only You*, Robert had been surrounded by drugs since childhood. His father has admitted introducing the actor to marijuana at the age of just six. By 1996, aged thirty-one, Robert was an addict, and in April of that year he was arrested for possession of cocaine, heroin and an unloaded gun while driving in Hollywood. It would be the first of many arrests over the next five years, years that included a four-month spell in jail in 1997, to almost a year in prison from 1999 to 2000. His career picked up when he was praised for his role in the TV series *Ally McBeal* following his release, but Robert was arrested again in 2000 for being in possession of cocaine and valium.

Like Lindsay's following her arrests, his career seemed to be collapsing, with projects cancelled (including his role in *Ally McBeal* and a proposed stage production of *Hamlet* to be directed by Mel Gibson) and the actor uninsurable. But when he completed rehab in 2001, the Hollywood community took another chance on him. First, he appeared in the memorable video for Elton John's single 'I Want Love', and then Mel Gibson offered to pay the insurance bond so Robert could appear in the movie *The Singing Detective*. More movie roles followed, and he received acclaim for his performances in thriller *Kiss Kiss Bang Bang* and David Fincher's superb *Zodiac*. It looked like the man whose career was once circling the drain was now a bona fide actor again, and in 2008 he became a megastar, following his terrific performance in the huge hit *Iron Man*. Clean, sober and at the top of his game, Robert Downey Jr was back, fulfilling the promise people first saw in his early movies. And with *Tropic Thunder* and *Sherlock Holmes* quickly following to both critical acclaim and box-office success, Robert was now not just a huge star, but a wonderful example of someone who had beaten their addictions and got their life back together again.

'He's an amazing actor,' Lindsay noted when comparisons with Robert were mentioned in a *Marie Claire* interview. 'Look at people like that, who have gone through shit and had to work that much harder to get where they are now. I've learned. I'll never go back. And it's not a never-say-never type thing.

'It's just – I know. I know.'

Chapter Nine
Living with the Lohans

As 2007 ended and 2008 began, it looked like Lindsay was putting the events of the past eighteen months behind her, and that she was ready to dust herself off and start over again. There were no bad boyfriends around her, only friends and family, and she was looking healthier than she had in a long while. Of course, the paparazzi continued to follow her, but instead of photos of her partying or passed out, instead they were getting pictures of her out visiting friends or shopping. In fact, when she popped into a Las Vegas radio station on 14 December 2007, hoping to get tickets to Hannah Montana for her friend's nieces (the station was running a competition giving tickets to anyone who could get a celebrity to call in), she ended up giving an impromptu interview on air with the morning show DJs.

'My life is different now, it's changed and I'm growing up,' the twenty-one-year-old actress said when asked about her recent troubles. 'It was time to grow up. I've gone through a lot, and I'm just a different person now.' She told the hosts that she wasn't going out partying any more, explaining why she hadn't been seen in the tabloids and added: 'It's amazing, everything's going so well.'

Lindsay also talked about her next project – a new album. 'I've been in the studio, it's going really well, and I'm really excited, 'cause it's going to be more urban pop,' she said. 'It's good to be back in the studio.' Her new album, tentatively titled *Spirit In the Dark*, had Lindsay on a new record label, Universal Motown, reportedly working with talents including Pharrell Williams (who has worked with Beyoncé, Britney Spears and Justin Timberlake) and singer-songwriter Ne-Yo (who has written and produced songs for Rihanna, Mariah Carey and Beyoncé).

It looked as if Lindsay was determined to get her life back on track and show the world how well she was doing. One way to do that was through photos, and Lindsay showed how fabulous she was looking and feeling when she posed on 5 February for a special set of photographs for the spring fashion edition of *New York* magazine. The photos were recreations of a very famous set of pictures taken more than four decades before, of Marilyn Monroe – the session, known as The Last Sitting, was taken by Bert Stern just six weeks before her death. The photos had been shot at the Hotel Bel-Air in 1962, and featured Marilyn, sleepy-eyed and nude except for a white sheet or piece of pink chiffon, looking beautiful, vulnerable and at times playful. The photos remained with Stern for more than twenty years, and when he did publish them, he included the photos that Marilyn had crossed out with a red pen, the ones she didn't like, and the images soon became iconic.

Lindsay had always had an affinity with Marilyn Monroe, Hollywood's most iconic, sexy actress, having first seen Marilyn in the movie *Niagara* when she was filming *The Parent Trap*.

Marilyn was, it could be argued, the first Hollywood star truly to live out her life under the tabloid glare, much as Lindsay would do fifty years later. Marilyn had had a difficult childhood, sometimes living with her mother, sometimes in foster care or with relatives, and she was married by the time she was sixteen. She was spotted by a photographer soon after, and began a career as a model that became more lucrative when she bleached her brunette hair blond. By the time she was twenty-one, she had divorced and was beginning a Hollywood career, first appearing in a non-speaking role in 1947's *The Shocking Miss Pilgrim*. It was her role in 1950's *The Asphalt Jungle* that truly launched her career, however, and by 1952 she had been described by *Life* magazine as 'the talk of Hollywood'. The press was on her trail too, when they discovered she was dating baseball player Joe DiMaggio, and everyone was fascinated by the personal life of the blond bombshell who appeared in such classics as the thriller *Niagara*, the musical *Gentlemen Prefer Blondes* and the comedy *How to Marry A Millionaire*.

The newspapers made it front-page news when Marilyn married Joe in 1954. She was now as big a star as he was, and she became even more famous that year when she appeared in the comedy *The Seven Year Itch*, featuring the iconic scene in which Marilyn's skirt blows up when she stands on a subway grate. Sadly, she and DiMaggio were divorced by the end of 1954, and she went on to film *Bus Stop* in the same year. Of course, it was many years before the internet, so when Marilyn then began a relationship with playwright Arthur Miller, the couple were able to keep it a secret for some time, but when the press found out, they were followed everywhere and dubbed 'the egghead and the hourglass'. In fact, things were almost as bad for them in terms of newspaper attention as they were for Lindsay years later – in 1956, a reporter following Marilyn and Arthur crashed his car, killing his female passenger.

Marilyn married Miller and went on to star in *The Prince and the Showgirl* and *Some Like It Hot* (where it was reported she was often late to set), followed by *Let's Make Love* and *The Misfits*. By now, newspapers were speculating that Marilyn was taking prescription drugs, and gossip columnists reported she was admitted to hospital for ten days in 1960 and was seeing a psychiatrist. She and Arthur divorced, and she was later hospitalised and underwent gall-bladder surgery.

In 1962 she was filming *Something's Got to Give*, but after only showing up on twelve days of the thirty-five-day shoot, she was asked to leave the movie. It was the last film she would make. A few weeks later, she posed for Bert Stern's photographs and discussed future projects with film-makers, including resuming filming on *Something's Got to Give*. Sadly, on 5 August 1962, Marilyn was found dead at her home in Brentwood, California, with the drugs chloral hydrate and Nembutal in her system. Her death was ruled as a possible suicide.

Lindsay had always been fascinated with this iconic, tragic film star, and in an interview with *New York* to accompany the photos, Lindsay talked about the Marilyn memorabilia she had at home, including a portrait of Marilyn that she was given one Christmas. 'It's eerie . . . it's this picture of her, and it's kind of cartoony. There's a big bottle of pills next to her, and they've fallen over.'

She talked about Marilyn's tragic death, and added: 'You know, it's also tragic what just recently happened to someone else,' referring to the death of Heath Ledger, who had died of an accidental drug overdose the month before. 'They are both prime examples of what this industry can do to someone.' Interviewer Amanda

Fortini then asked Lindsay if she thought she might meet a similar tragic fate. 'I don't know. I'm not them. But I sure as hell wouldn't let it happen to me.'

For the photo shoot, *New York* asked Bert Stern to recreate his photos of Marilyn, so he decided to shoot Lindsay on film rather than with a digital camera. She was happy to accept the challenge. 'I didn't have to put much thought into it. I mean, Bert Stern? Doing a Marilyn shoot? When is that ever going to come up? It's really an honour.' Of course, this did mean Lindsay would have to pose nude ('I was comfortable with it,' she said, adding that she did '250 crunches' the night before), and also wear a blond wig to recreate her idol. (Three platinum-blond wigs were tried before the stylist found one that truly made Lindsay look like Marilyn).

'It was very similar, déjà vu you might say, like revisiting an old street,' Stern said of the shoot with Lindsay. The shoot was soon being mentioned in newspapers around the world, with the *New York Times* saying that 'Ms Lohan looks narrow-hipped and voluptuous in the pictures, taut and soft,' but the fact the shots were nude did cause some controversy. Lindsay was pleased with the results, however, as she told Lauren Hutton in *Interview* a few months later. 'When I did that shoot, people didn't frown on it. People were like, "That's a bold thing to do." People looked at that shoot more than they've looked at any film I've done in the past four or five years.'

Dina Lohan approved of the photos, as she told *People*. 'I looked at it as art, and as Lindsay doing a character. So I don't look at them like it's *Playboy*; she was being a character. If you look at it that way, you can look at it as a mother. Of course we talked about how they would be done. Lindsay said, "Mommy, I'm never going to get this opportunity to do it again." She was very thankful she was asked.'

Lindsay's father was less than impressed, however. 'I'm not going to look at the photos – that's my daughter!' he told *Us Weekly*. 'I pray there are no parallels to her and Marilyn Monroe's destiny.'

He had been unhappy with previous photos Lindsay had posed for, too. While he was in prison in 2007, Lindsay had posed for men's magazine *Maxim*, and Michael told reporter Spencer Morgan that his fellow inmates would stick up the sexy photos from the shoot, and other provocative photos of his daughter, and write words like 'slut', 'whore' and 'bitch' on them.

He probably wasn't too fond of Lindsay's next project, either. Along with friend Samantha Ronson and Kanye West, she appeared in the video for N.E.R.D's latest single, 'Everyone Nose'. It was filmed in a New York club called Madison on 2 April, with one hundred partygoers as extras, and attracted controversy even while it was being filmed. MTV reported that a fight broke out during filming between two male extras, hours after both the band and Lindsay had left the shoot. 'I think the whole fight was about getting more camera time,' James Demasi, one of the managers of the club, said. 'I was there, and the fight was between two males. One of them was taunting the other, and the extra who was being taunted jumped up and assaulted the individual who was taunting him. Some of the glass props broke, and the extra who was behind the attack fell down with the other guy, and cut his arm on the broken glass he fell on. They were pulled apart, and the guy who was attacked went to the hospital.'

The song had been controversial even before the fight during the video shoot, as there are references in the lyrics to cocaine, and for a while MTV refused to play it until a cleaner version was available. Lindsay only appeared briefly in the video, her face just one of many images of people clubbing.

Her own music career was back on track, too. On 7 May, Lindsay released a new single, 'Bossy', written by Ne-Yo and production team Stargate (a Norwegian duo known for their work with Rihanna). 'I wrote it for her because when she's on her game, you can see these traits in her. When she's focused, she exudes the aura of a boss with ease,' Ne-Yo told *People*. 'When Stargate and I were approached with the task, we viewed it as a challenge. "Can we make a song for Lindsay Lohan that people were gonna take seriously?" I think we did it. It's basically about a woman being strong enough to get what she wants when she wants it. In this case, "Bossy" is a term that describes confidence and power.'

In an interview with *Billboard*, Ne-Yo said he was surprised to be asked to work on a track for Lindsay. 'I gotta admit, we were like . . . *Lindsay Lohan*?' he said. 'I mean, I've written for Beyoncé, Mary J. Blige, Rihanna, Celine Dion and . . . Lindsay Lohan? But I will say this; we gave her a quality record and she did a ridiculously fabulous job. I was so shocked I had to call her and apologise for what I was thinking because she did so good. I think the world is gonna be surprised.'

The song went to number one on *Billboard*'s Hot Dance Club Play chart, and received good reviews with digitalspy.co.uk calling it 'electro dance-pop with attitude'.

Lindsay also had her first acting job since her recovery. It wasn't a movie, but a guest role in the hit TV series *Ugly Betty*. The series had begun two years before, in September 2006, and had become an instant hit. Based on a Colombian telenovela called *Yo Soy Betty La Fea*, the American version was produced by, among others, actress Salma Hayek.

Ugly Betty followed the adventures of Betty Suarez (America Ferrera), a young Mexican woman from Queens with braces on her teeth, a bad haircut and even worse fashion sense. Wanting to be a journalist, she accepts a job on the fashion magazine *Mode*, whose new editor is womaniser Daniel Meade (Eric Mabius). Daniel's father Bradford hires Betty to be Daniel's assistant, as he knows she's the one woman his son won't try to seduce, and she might actually help him keep the magazine going. There are trials at work for them both, however, as creative director Wilhelmina Slater (Vanessa Williams) wants Daniel's job, while her assistant Mark (Michael Urie) and bitchy receptionist Amanda (Becki Newton) take it in turns to make Betty's life hell by mocking her lack of taste.

Lindsay appeared in four episodes of the show, beginning with 'Jump', which was broadcast on 22 May. She starred as Kimmie Keegan, an old school mate of Betty, who was horrible to her at school and is not much nicer when their paths cross as adults. It was only a brief appearance, but Lindsay went on to costar in the episodes 'The Manhattan Project' (in which Betty discovers Kimmie is her dad's boss at his new job in a burger bar), 'Granny Pants' (where Betty hires Kimmie as her temporary assistant, only to see Kimmie get promoted above her) and 'Ugly Berry' (in which Kimmie gets her comeuppance).

Originally scheduled to appear in six episodes during season two and three of *Ugly Betty*, Lindsay only appeared in four, among rumours of a feud between her and the series' star, America Ferrera. 'I think it's hysterical,' co-star Becki Newton told MTV News of the gossip. 'It's like right out of a script for *Ugly Betty*.'

She went on to say: 'We had a great time shooting [with Lindsay]. I'm not sure how many episodes she did, but if you watch the show, you'll see that her storyline ended exactly the way it was supposed to end, and we had a great experience filming with her.

I'm clearing the air that real life is never as interesting as the drama people make up.'

'America is grateful to have had [Lindsay] on the show, and thinks everyone should tune in to see how great the episodes are,' America Ferrera's publicist told the *New York Post*, who had originally published the rumours. Lindsay's publicist added that: 'Lindsay was scheduled for six episodes and is appearing in four but had a lovely time.'

Co-star Vanessa Williams praised Lindsay's performance to *OK!*. 'I think she did a really good job. People will be pleased. She makes a great transition from Kimmie, who is working at Flushing Burger, to working for me at *Mode*, and people will enjoy seeing her progress.' Lindsay loved working there, too, writing on her MySpace page: 'It's been such a delight to be a part of this show. I am quite sad to have to leave the wonderful cast and crew behind. It's always sad to leave people that you get close to.'

While Lindsay's fans – and many more besides – tuned into the *Ugly Betty* episodes, there was another show featuring the Lohan name that was making its debut on TV, but this time it was nothing to do with Lindsay. *Living Lohan*, a reality series broadcast on the E! Entertainment channel in the US, debuted on 26 May and documented the daily lives of Lindsay's mother, Dina, and the rest of the family, including Lindsay's fourteen-year-old sister Ali, who was attempting to break into show business at the time, brother

Cody and Dina's mother Ann (Nana). Before the series launched, Dina made it clear her eldest daughter would not be involved.

'I told Lindsay I don't want her on the show right now. Doing reality TV would almost be taking a step backward as far as her career is concerned,' she said in an interview with World Entertainment Network News. 'I did this to defuse the rumours about my family. The media has been so horrific to us over the past two years. I just want to get the message across that we are a normal family.'

Each of the series' nine episodes followed the family's highs and lows, beginning with the first episode 'Mommy Will Fix It', in which Dina was seen reading tabloid reports about both Ali and Lindsay, including one speculating that there is a sex tape of Lindsay on the Internet. The episode also followed Ali as she learned she was going to record her first album at the Palms Casino in Las Vegas (perhaps not coincidentally owned by Gavin and Phil Maloof, who were also the producers of *Living Lohan*).

Episode two was called 'Burning Down the House', and included Dina and Ali rowing with music producer Jeremy Greene about Ali's album, and Dina appearing at a party for *Boulevard*, who had run an interview with her back in 2006. Episode three, 'Mean Girls', followed Ali as she was bullied at school and taught by her mother how to handle reporters, while part four, 'Like Mother Like Daughter', had Ali begging for – and getting – a puppy of her own despite the family having five dogs already, and Dina's son Michael Jr coming home from college with his girlfriend, only for them all to have a huge argument.

The final five episodes, entitled 'Grandma Won't Budge', 'Moving to Las Vegas!', 'The Billionaire Babysitters', 'Show Girls' and 'Acting Up' focused on the family's move to Las Vegas while Ali recorded her album, and Ali's attempts to launch an acting career. In an interview with *Teen Vogue*, she spoke of wanting to have a life like her sister's.

'I grew up watching Lindsay,' she said. 'It made me want to do what she does. Just the whole vibe. Being there, being on camera, or on stage, with everybody listening to you . . . it's so cool when people look up to you. I've already been asked for my autograph, and it's just a really good feeling to have.'

Unfortunately for Ali, the press didn't like the series. *Entertainment Weekly*'s Gillian Flynn gave the show an F grade and wrote: '[Dina] invites us to gape at her, Lindsay's fourteen-year-old fame-seeking sis Ali and eleven-year-old Cody. And hey, it turns out I *don't* want to Live Lohan. The irritation turned to repulsion around the first minute, when Dina, after her morning ritual of scanning the tabloids for Lindsay's weary mug, announces: "They'd better not start in on Ali like this." Hey, I have an idea: *Don't film a reality show in your child's fricking bedroom!*

'The woman who last year told *Harper's Bazaar*,

Lindsay Lohan with her brother Cody in New York, taking a
break from shooting a music video.

(Photo by Arnaldo Magnani/Getty Images)

Left: Lindsay Lohan and Harry Morton.
(Photo by Jeff Vespa/WireImage)

Below: Ali Lohan, Lindsay Lohan, Cody Lohan and Michael Lohan Jr at Lindsay Lohan's 21st birthday.
(Photo by Kevin Mazur/WireImage)

Right: Lindsay Lohan shooting a print commercial in LA.
(Photo by Todd Williamson/ WireImage)

Lindsay Lohan with America
Ferrera filming for *Ugly Betty*
in New York City.

(Photo by James Devaney/WireImage)

Above: Press outside Lindsay Lohan and Samantha Ronson's Hollywood home.
(Photo by David Aguilera/BuzzFoto/FilmMagic)

Right: Lindsay Lohan and Samantha Ronson.
(Photo by Stephen Lovekin/Getty Images for IMG)

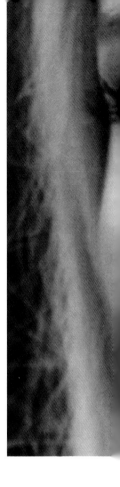

Above left: Karl Lagerfeld
and Lindsay Lohan.
(Photo by Dominique Charriau/
WireImage)

Below left: Lindsay
Lohan and Ali Lohan.
(Photo by Jean Baptiste Lacroix/
WireImage)

Lindsay Lohan reveals her
controversial fingernail at
her probation revocation
hearing on 6 July 2010.
(Photo by David McNew/Getty Images)

Left: Lindsay Lohan breaks down in court – with lawyer Shawn Chapman Holley at her probation revocation hearing.

(Photo by David McNew/Getty Images)

Below: The Gottis: *Three Generations* press conference.

(Photo by D. Dipasupil/FilmMagic)

"Reality shows, I get sick inside," now invites cameras to document the launch of Ali's singing career . . . The remainder of the Lohans' lives apparently revolves around Googling themselves, watching tabloid TV and then having an assistant Google more. Mother Lohan defends this gossip-gathering as protecting her daughters, but there's an uncomfortable sheen of glee to the proceedings. "Is that Lindsay?" young Ali says, looking over her mother's shoulder at a still from a sex tape starring a Lindsay lookalike; she seems more curious than upset. (Lindsay has wisely ducked out of this fiasco – not even her voice is heard on the phone.) Dina snipes about the paparazzi's invasion of privacy, but thanks to her, there's not too much left to invade.'

Other critics agreed with Flynn, and CNN journalist Anderson Cooper also started a war of words with Dina Lohan when he guest-hosted popular US morning show *Live With Regis and Kelly*, criticising Dina and the show on air, commenting that Ali 'looks to be about 60 . . . I say that with concern and love', and saying, 'I can't believe I'm wasting a minute of my life watching these horrific people.'

Dina quickly responded, telling *OK!* that: 'people are just cruel . . . this is bad karma for him', while Dina's ex-husband Michael also commented to *Access Hollywood*, 'I think Anderson Cooper is an opinionated, hypocritical idiot who should be an adult and keep his opinion to himself. He is the last person to judge anyone, when he and his own family have their issues.' Anderson made one final comment about the affair. 'Let me just reiterate, I feel bad for the fourteen-year-old daughter. She seems like a nice person, but she should be a kid, not in a [reality show],' he said in a statement.

A second series of the show was never made, with Dina commenting in 2009 to *Life & Style* magazine that it was her decision to do the show and also to end it. 'I only did the show to defuse the rumours. And then they wanted us to do these crazy things, like my son cheating on his girlfriend, me faking a pregnancy. I was like, "No, no, no!" They had ideas that weren't conducive to our ideas.'

Asked if she would do another reality show, she added: 'We're working with another network on another idea. Not reality per se, but a realistic show.' (In March 2010, Dina announced another show was in the works, but nothing has appeared as yet.)

The series may have lasted just nine episodes, but there were more Lohan family secrets soon to be revealed to the public, whether Lindsay liked it or not. In June 2008, it emerged that Michael had had an affair in 1995 (when he was separated from Dina) with a Montana massage therapist named Kristi Kaufman, and she was now claiming that he was the father of her thirteen-year-old daughter Ashley.

In an interview with *OK!*, Kristi talked about her decision to go public with the story: '**Many times I offered to do this privately so the other Lohan kids** wouldn't be hurt. But Michael would not live up to his obligations.'

On 30 June, Michael submitted to a paternity test ('If the test is found to be negative, she's gonna be sued for libel and defamation,' he told the *New York Post* the next day) and revealed he had known about Ashley's existence since 2005, after Kristi contacted him while he was in prison.

'She contacted me and said she had a paternity test with her ex-husband and it was negative and she believed the child was mine,' Michael told the newspaper. 'She said I was the only one she was with, but I find that hard to believe. She was with a number of men after me, and is going through a second divorce right now.'

Michael was also critical of the fact that Kristi had gone to the press with the story. 'Even if the test is positive, I have nothing to say to her because of the way she handled this,' he said. 'How can someone say I have another child when no testing has been done? Why did she wait so long? Is it because she wants money? Or is it because she wants to claim that Ashley is my children's sister? She said she wants her daughter to have a relationship with my kids – especially Lindsay and Ali – and that's pretty sick.'

The matter remained unresolved for some time, with Kaufman applying for child support from Michael Lohan for her daughter. According to Radar-Online, in 2010 Michael asked Kristi to appear with him on the chat show *The Maury Povich Show* to do a DNA test, and she refused. 'For the third time, Kristi has declined. Tell me, if Kristi is so sure, and she even had the nerve to change Ashley's birth certificate to my last name, why won't she [let Ashley] take the test?

'We are going to reopen the case,' Michael added, talking about a ruling that asked him to pay Kaufman $300,000 in child support. 'And demand a paternity test. What nerve this three-times-scorned con woman has to have her daughter claim she is my daughter, without any proof and not wanting to find out the truth for herself.'

By November 2010, Ashley Kaufman's paternity caused Michael Lohan legal problems when it emerged he had missed a child support payment (he had not contested a court case asking him to make regular payments to Ashley's mother, even though it had yet to be established whether he was the father).

Lindsay wrote about it all on her MySpace page at the end of 2008. 'People go through a lot in life. And the things that we go through, whatever they may be, simply just make us stronger in the long run . . . That is, if we actually take what it is we have learned from our mistakes and teach ourselves what *not* to do in the future. I have gone through a lot in my past, and to be completely honest, I am still going through a lot right now. My father just let my family and I know, among others, that he had another child after my little sister

Aliana, or maybe he had it before Aliana? Either way, he cheated on my mother, and that really sucks . . .'

She later told Lucy Kaylin of *Marie Claire*: 'I don't know what's going on with it. I haven't asked him any questions. Apparently, we've been in the dark for so many years. We've gone through enough with him. Enough is enough.' She revealed that she was cutting off contact with her father 'until he decides to be a grown-up'.

While the whole paternity issue must have been deeply upsetting for Lindsay, it also affected the girl at the centre of the storm, Ashley. She told *Life & Style* in 2010 how she felt about the man who could be her father. 'I do not trust him, and I don't want to be around him or to be part of his life. I could never call Michael Lohan "Dad". A dad is a person who is there for you and takes care of you.'

Relations between Lindsay and her father had once again broken down, but she picked herself up and focused on two new projects instead, a charity called Visa Swap and the launch of her own clothes line, 6126.

Visa Swap is an ethical swap sale, which actress Mischa Barton had been the face of in 2007. 'The idea is that people take their unwanted, or unwise, fashion purchases to a temporary shop in Knightsbridge, London and swap them with other people,' Mischa explained at the time. 'I love trading clothes with friends, and it's a great way to get new looks while offloading stuff you're bored of. I love the environmental side of it; nothing is wasted.'

For the 2008 sale held in London's Covent Garden in June, Lindsay donated an Issa dress, a pair of Jimmy Choo shoes, a Miu Miu bag and two vintage outfits that included a silver shift dress. 'Usually I hate giving away clothes,' she told Christa D'Souza of *The Times* newspaper. 'Everything I wear, it has such personality, but I think this is an amazing idea, so I'm more than willing to give what I can.'

Anything unsold from the celebrity donations is given to the clothes recycling charity TRAID. They recycle the best items to be sold in their shops, with damaged items remade into new one-off pieces, sold under the charity's fashion label TRAIDremade. The charity's aim is to protect the environment by diverting clothes and shoes from landfill; to reduce world poverty by raising funds for overseas development projects; and to educate the UK public on environmental and world poverty issues.

The following month, Lindsay set about launching her own fashion line, named 6126. The name had special significance for Lindsay, as it was the birth date of Marilyn Monroe (1 June 1926). 'As most of you know, 6126 is named after Marilyn Monroe's birth date. Marilyn is the ultimate icon. She represents timeless, confident glamour, which I hope that 6126 designs always reflect,' Lindsay wrote on the fashion line's website. The collection launched in July 2008 with a series of leggings designs, including 'Dom' black leggings with a side zip at the ankle for $123 and leopard-print 'ankle gloves' for $42.

Lindsay was 6126's creative director and designed the leggings with president of the company Kristi Taylor, who worked with a five-person team with Lindsay always heavily involved. 'She approves everything, down to invitations for events,' Kristi said in an interview for the *LA Times*, adding to *Women's Wear Daily* magazine: 'She's not a celebrity who lends her name to a brand. She's intimately involved from Day One. She picks fabrics. She looks at trims. She picks buttons. She doesn't let anything go into production without trying it on.'

6126 was instantly a hit, with the leggings originally being sold in Fred Segal stores ('there's not much you can do with leggings, but I'm doing everything I can', Lindsay told *Harper's Bazaar* in an interview after the collection launched). In 2010, it was announced the label was going to expand beyond just leggings, with Lindsay writing on 6126's website on 1 July: 'I am so excited for the entire 6126 ready-to-wear collection to be hitting stores and available to U on our website. I was so proud of the 6126 legging line and it was truly time to expand into a full collection. I really had a great time designing and being a part of the entire process. 6126 is Classic, Sexy and Glamorous. I want women to feel good about themselves wearing it. It is both elegant and glamorous with a sexy edge. Very soon you will be able to purchase 6126 dresses, leather jackets, blazers, coats, mini and pencil skirts, blouses and corsets for the first time in materials such as cashmere, silk, leather, chiffon and lace.'

'The goal is to build the ultimate lifestyle brand based on classic glamour with a fashion twist,' Kristi Taylor told the *LA Times* in 2010. '[Lindsay's] very engaged. It's such a different thing when you sit with her. You get a sense of her passion about fashion . . . I believe she will always be there for the brand. At the end of the day, she has a heart of gold. She just needs people to believe in her.'

The line, which is expected to expand into make-up and handbags, is now sold at big American department stores such as Neiman Marcus and Bloomingdale's, Kitson in Japan and Harrods in the UK, with Lindsay and her sister Ali both modelling for the label's advertising campaigns. Wikipedia estimates its current worth at an impressive $3 million.

At last, it looked like Lindsay had something to celebrate and, as she revealed in July 2008, someone to celebrate with . . .

Chapter Ten
Samantha

For the previous few months, the tabloid press had been
speculating that there was someone new in Lindsay's
life. At first, everyone thought Samantha Ronson was
just a friend (she had been in the car on one of the
occasions Lindsay had crashed), but as 2008 began,
people started to wonder whether she was Lindsay's
new love.

Samantha couldn't have been more different than
Lindsay. Born on 7 August 1977 (making her nine years
older than Lindsay) in London, she is the daughter of
ex-Bucks Fizz band manager Laurence Ronson and
socialite Ann Dexter-Jones, and is descended from
Eastern European Jewish families. Samantha counts

former British Home Secretary Leon Brittan and former Foreign Secretary Malcolm Rifkind among her distant relatives, and she also has a twin sister, Charlotte (now a fashion designer), and an older brother, Mark, who has a successful DJ-ing, recording and producing career, having produced some of both Lily Allen's and Amy Winehouse's most memorable songs.

Samantha's parents split when she was four, and her mother Ann moved the family to New York. Ann later married Mick Jones, founder of the rock band Foreigner, and their relationship is believed to have inspired the hit song 'I Want To Know What Love Is'. The family, which now included a stepbrother and stepsister from her mother's remarriage (plus three more stepsiblings from her father's second marriage), was surrounded by music – the children were friends with Liv Tyler (now a famous actress, of course, and daughter of Aerosmith singer Steven Tyler), and brother Mark's best friend growing up was Sean Lennon, son of John Lennon and Yoko Ono. Daryl Hall, Paul McCartney and Bruce Springsteen all visited the family home while Samantha was growing up, so it is no surprise that she turned to music as a potential career, just like her older brother.

Her first foray into music was in a rap band called The Low Lifes when she was sixteen years old. Mother Ann had strict rules about her young daughter's social life, however, and she told the *New York Times* that all her kids had to go to bed at a normal time every night, unless there was a party at their own home. 'We let them stay up. We just kept the bar out of bounds.'

When Samantha finished high school, she spent a year in Paris and then returned to New York, teaching herself to play and sing music. 'I had [Del Rios'] "Macarena" and like, a Motown box set and I was like, "I've got to do something,"' Ronson told MTV. 'I had a guitar that my dad had given me, hanging on the wall, and I just started playing and I was just like, "Ah, this is love." It made me realise why [my stepfather and brother] did the things they'd done. I was like, "I gotta be a part of it . . . it's so much fun."'

She eventually got into the music business not as a singer-songwriter, but as a DJ. 'I got a call one night from a club that I used to hang out at and they were like, "Do you want to DJ?"' Ronson remembered on her website. 'I was like, "No way," [but] my friends were like, "Come on, just do it. How hard could it be?" I was always in the club; [I figured I] might as well get paid for it.'

That first DJ-ing gig led to more and more, and in 2001 she was asked to spin the discs for MTV's New Year's Eve party in Times Square. Then, she became the first rock act to be signed to hip-hop label Roc-A-Fella, and began working with producers including her brother Mark, singer Duncan Sheik and Dallas Austin (Pink) to make her first album. 'When I first started doing music stuff it was really folky and acoustic because that was what I was listening to at the time,' she told MTV in 2003. 'And then I started thinking about, "Well, do I want to be that girl playing on a stool, with, like, flowers and candles, or do I want to have a fun record?" And as I got more and more into hip-hop, I was like, "Oh, let's have loops and let's make it more fun and let's make it move."'

That album was called *Red*, and featured a song called 'Built This Way' that, coincidentally, ended up appearing in Lindsay's movie *Mean Girls*, two years before she and Lindsay would actually meet in person. *Red* was never officially released, but appeared on Samantha's MySpace page. She returned her focus to DJ-ing, splitting her time between New York and LA, and it was there that she met Lindsay.

Their friendship first came to light in the press in 2007, as Samantha was a passenger in Lindsay's car when the actress was arrested for drink-driving and possession of cocaine. Within days, bloggers were writing nasty things about the press-shy DJ, and she decided to sue to get retractions for the comments (gossip blogger Perez Hilton, for example, described her as a 'lezbot DJ' and wore a T-shirt on his blog that had 'Blame Samantha' on the front, and, unfortunately, this particular case ended in a protracted legal battle.

Journalists started to wonder whether Samantha and Lindsay were more than just friends in 2008, with Kate Aurthur of the *Los Angeles Times* writing on 20 July 2008 that gossip columnists were reporting a romance between the women. 'Neither Lohan nor

Ronson has spoken to the media about their relationship, and not surprisingly, Lohan's publicist would not comment for this story nor make Lohan herself available, writing in an email that Lohan "wants to keep her private life private". (Ronson likewise did not respond to a request for comment made through her website),' Aurthur wrote.

In an interview with *Marie Claire* in the summer of 2008, writer Lucy Kaylin wrote that Lindsay refused to confirm she and Samantha were lovers, though she noted Lindsay often mentioned the DJ in conversation. 'Samantha has a bunch of stars, so I got that,' Lindsay said of a tattoo on her hand, and she also mentioned buying a house 'with someone'. When Kaylin specifically asked Lindsay about her relationship with Sam, however, she replied: 'People can think what they want. I'm really happy, and that's all that matters.'

'She's a great person,' Lindsay added when asked about Samantha's influence on her life. 'And she's a great influence on the people around her. But I think that anything that's changed in my life is because of me. I've gone through it, and I've had to deal with it, and I've made the decision to move forward. So yeah, she's a great person.'

The press went wild on 23 September when it appeared that Lindsay had confessed to a relationship with Sam on the radio show *Loveline*. Samantha was being interviewed over the phone, and she handed the phone to Lindsay. Radio host Stryker asked her how long she and Samantha had been dating, and after a pause, Lindsay answered: 'A very long time.' Then, when the host complimented the pair by saying they were a great-looking couple and he hoped they would stay together, she replied, 'Thank you very much.'

Lindsay's dad Michael, once again estranged from her, was not impressed by this new revelation about his daughter's personal life. He sent an email to X17 Online to let his feelings about Samantha be known just days after their relationship became more public, commenting on remarks on Lindsay's MySpace page that defended her friend and criticising his daughter for supporting Samantha when her friends, including DJ AM, were hospitalised after surviving a plane crash on 19 September.

Lindsay replied by releasing a statement to newspaper gossip column Page Six. 'My father obviously needs to be on medication to control his moods. He is out of line, and his words show how much anger he has, and it's dangerous and scary as it reminds me of how he treated my mother and I my whole childhood. He needs to be stopped. This is yet another reason why we aren't speaking.

'I am in a great place in life,' Lindsay continued. 'I have overcome a lot and have been able to learn how to enjoy and appreciate my life in every way possible. I'm proud of myself for being able to make a change in the past year and a half. My past is behind me, and that's final. There's nothing more to be said. All the false accusations that people try to make are simply because there's no story when things are calm and good. But they might as well let it go because their lies don't affect me any more. Samantha is not evil, I care for her very much and she's a wonderful girl.

'She loves me, as I do her.'

Their relationship was now public, and in an interview published in November 2008 with *Harper's Bazaar*, while Lindsay was reluctant to reveal anything about Sam, she did eventually talk about it. 'I feel like it jinxes it,' she told reporter Marshall Heyman about talking about relationships. 'It's hard. The second I start talking about whomever I'm seeing, a month or two later it's failed.' Heyman mentioned to Lindsay that she had been photographed out and about with Samantha a lot, including on holiday in Mexico, to which she replied: 'It's pretty obvious who I'm seeing. It's no shock to anyone that it's been going on for quite some time . . . She's a wonderful person and I love her very much.'

Lindsay also opened up about her sexuality in the interview. When asked if she was bisexual, she answered: 'Maybe. Yeah,' and replied 'No' when asked if she was a lesbian. 'I don't want to classify myself. First of all, you never know what's going to happen – tomorrow, in a month, a year from now, five years from now. I appreciate people, and it doesn't matter who they are. I feel blessed to be able to feel comfortable enough with myself that I can say that.'

Her mother and siblings were supportive of her relationship, too. 'It's never really come up as an issue,' she said. 'We're close, we've been through a lot. They're supportive of me whether I'm with a guy or a girl. They're just supportive of me as a person. Ali's known Samantha for a really long time. And she's like, "Whatever it is, I support you. I probably won't ever do what it is you're doing, but I'm happy for you." Ali's very mature. I've told her that it's OK to like a boy or a girl if you're comfortable with it and it's something you believe you want to do. I told her not to be afraid of who she wants to be.'

It sounded like Lindsay had grown up and become wiser and happier, too. Another change in her life came behind the scenes as she stopped her mother managing her business affairs, replacing her with friend Jenni Muro. In an interview in *Marie Claire* with Lindsay, reporter Lucy Kaylin described Muro as 'shrewd' and 'protective', and also 'strategic – for instance, welcoming paparazzi shots of Lohan on the set, working [as opposed to tumbling out of a club].'

Muro, a survivor of ovarian cancer, was another good influence on Lindsay's life. 'When I open the window and breathe the air, that's a good day,' Muro said. 'All this crap doesn't matter. Life is much bigger than that. I share my perspective with her [Lindsay], and I don't think anyone else has really done that.' Muro was with Lindsay on set during the summer of

2008 while the actress was working on her first film since *Chapter 27* – a comedy called *Labor Pains*.

Lindsay stars as Thea Clayhill, secretary to grumpy publisher Jerry (comedian Chris Parnell). She thinks she is about to lose her job, so she lies and tells her boss she is expecting a baby, because she saw on an episode of *Law & Order* that it is discriminatory to fire a pregnant woman. Thea fakes her pregnancy with the help of a fake baby bump, but when her boss's cute brother Nick (Luke Kirby) comes to work at the office, things start getting complicated. Nick wants her to head up the new parenting division at the publishing company, which means both a promotion and a raise, and a romantic relationship looks like it may start between Nick and Thea, too. But how will she be able to keep pretending she's pregnant when she and Nick are getting closer?

The directorial debut of Lara Shapiro, the movie filmed from 9 June to 18 July in Burbank, California. During production, producer Lati Grobman told *People* why she took a chance on Lindsay when others wouldn't cast her in their movies. 'She's so natural at what she does,' Grobman said of Lindsay. 'I've never seen one take where she's off. The difference between her and the other girls that are naughty in the business is that she's actually talented.'

Director Shapiro, meanwhile, gave an interview to *Movieline* magazine about working with Lindsay. 'We basically wrote it [the movie] with her in mind. There are not many people that can do what she does. The very earliest script we wrote reflected the same kind of attitudes and general character. Lindsay has an incredible ability to make the audience really sympathise with her, and that was something that was important to us. That the character not be someone that you're turned off by because the choices that she's making are not that great. But still you have to be rooting for her and understanding what she's doing.'

Knowing that the paparazzi would hound Lindsay during filming, Shapiro and her team came up with a plan. 'We shot in Burbank and we had a core set of about five locations that were all within a block of each other that were all owned by the same company. So we rented out the offices and the apartment, and as a result we were able to keep things as sane as possible. There were only a couple days when we were really bothered by the paparazzi, like in a baseball scene. We were shooting the scene in the outfield and there were paparazzi in the shot. And then there was another day where Cheryl and Lindsay were coming out of the maternity store. That was stressful because we were running out of light. They had a page and a half of dialogue and we were running out of time to shoot it. I was standing next to three paparazzi. Then there were four on the other side of the camera. They were really in her face.'

It seemed everyone wanted to get a photo of Lindsay, whatever she was doing, and once her relationship with

Samantha was out in the open, the couple were followed all the time. Press reports appeared daily speculating that they had either broken up or made up. Unfortunately, all the press attention proved detrimental when Lindsay volunteered to campaign on behalf of presidential candidate Barack Obama in the run-up to the election.

On 17 September, the *Chicago Sun-Times* reported that Lindsay had offered to host a series of events aimed at younger voters, but her offer was declined. According to the newspaper, a source in the Obama camp told them that Lindsay 'is not exactly the kind of high-profile star who would be a positive for us'. Nonetheless, Lindsay did continue to show her political support for the Democratic candidate, writing about him on her MySpace page, where she also criticised Sarah Palin, the extremely conservative running mate of Republican Senator John McCain, who has often expressed her anti-same-sex marriage and anti-abortion stance. 'I really cannot bite my tongue any more when it comes to Sarah Palin,' she wrote. 'Is it a sin to be gay? Should it be a sin to be straight? Or to use birth control? Or to have sex before marriage? Or even to have a child out of wedlock?'

'I have faith that this country will be all that it can be with the proper guidance. I really hope that all of you make your decisions based on the facts and what feels right to you in your heart. Vote for Obama!' At the end of her posting, Lindsay wrote: 'I am not against

Sarah Palin as a mother or a woman. In the words of Pamela Anderson: "She can suck it!"'

2008 was coming to an end, but before it did, Lindsay announced to her fans that she had not yet completed her third album, and the single, 'Bossy', she had released earlier in the year would be her last recording for a while. On 13 November, in an interview with *Access Hollywood*, she said: 'I just got off the phone with my Motown manager. I've been avoiding calling her back. I just – I didn't want to. With my other records, I kind of just did it, just to do it.' She explained that she didn't want to be working on more than one project at a time, so the album was on the back burner. However, by February 2010, there was still no sign of a forthcoming record release, and, when asked, producer-writer Ne-Yo, who had been working with Lindsay, told PoptArt magazine: 'We were doing some stuff and then it just fell off and hasn't got back on. I'm not gonna hold my breath.'

In the meantime, Lindsay considered a series of projects, and was also seen around New York and Los Angeles with Samantha. They made headlines once again on New Year's Eve, following reports over the previous few weeks that they had been fighting. On 31 December, Sam was DJ-ing at the Mansion club in Miami's South Beach, when onlookers reported she and Lindsay started yelling at each other. The fight was recorded by someone on a phone and posted on the Internet, once again showing that nothing in Lindsay's life was private. Newspapers printed stories saying the couple had broken up, but on 5 January, Lindsay posted a message on her MySpace page saying, 'Little piece of TRUE information, we did NOT break up!'

Over the next few months, the press followed the couple in the hope of catching them in the middle of an argument. In the end, on 6 April 2009, Lindsay announced to E! News that they had split – 'We are taking a brief break so I can focus on myself.' Just two days later, it was reported that Samantha's family had visited the police, asking about obtaining a restraining order to stop Lindsay having any contact with her ex. 'On Monday 6 April 2009, at approximately 5 p.m., members of Samantha Ronson's family came to the Beverly Hills Police Department,' a police spokesperson told *The Huffington Post*. 'They were given information for the process of obtaining a restraining order, which will be administered at the Santa Monica Superior Courthouse.'

Realising that all the speculation about her love life was getting bizarre, Lindsay even recorded a spoof advert for dating agency eHarmony, for the comedy website Funny Or Die. The ad had Lindsay talking to the camera about who she is, and what she looks for in a mate:

My name is Lindsay and I'm searching for love. I'm recently single, I think, and I'm looking for someone who I can spend the rest of my life with. Or, at least the rest of my probation with. Ha ha. A little bit about me. I'm an actress, a singer, an entrepreneur and I single-handedly kept ninety per cent of all gossip websites in business. I would define my personality as, uh, creative. I'm a bit of a night owl. I'm a workaholic, a shopaholic and, according to the state of California, an alcoholic, as well as a threat to all security guards if they work at hotels. And to put all those rumours to rest, I am not broke. I actually have over four hundred dollars in the bank and twenty thousand Marlboro Milds, which I'm very proud of.

I'm looking for a compatible mate who likes a night out on the town, as long as he or she is driving, of course. Likes ankle-monitoring bracelets, and doesn't have family members quick to issue restraining orders. The perfect mate loves long walks on the beach, car chases on the PCH, antiquing, and, uh, passing out in Cadillac Escalades. So if you think you can handle a redhead with a little bit of sass – and by that I mean a redhead that's crazy. I mean, don't pretend like you don't know me. We've all read about it. We'll crash a few parties, a car or two, but at the end of the day, I promise you I never lose my Google hits, just my underwear . . .'

Despite all the negative press, Lindsay remained busy. She launched her own self-tanning spray, Sevin Nyne (named after Lindsay's lucky numbers, 7 and 9), on 1 May, through beauty retailer Sephora, with the product getting great reviews. *Daily Telegraph* reporter Melissa Whitworth tried it out and commented: 'I woke up with a tan that was as close to the colour my skin goes in the sun as I've ever seen. There were no streaks or patches, just a warm glow that looked completely natural and lasted all weekend.'

Lindsay created the spray with celebrity airbrush tanner Lorit Simon. 'We wanted to create something without harsh chemicals or dyes that nourished the skin and inspired people to cherish their skin and stay out of the sun,' said Simon. 'I have pale skin, so sitting in the sun was never an option. I was frustrated with the tanning formulas on the market so I decided to create my own. We wanted everyone to enjoy a professional spray tan in the privacy of their own home, and I think we succeeded.' There was some controversy after the tanning spray was released: chemist Jennifer Sunday accused Lindsay and Lorit of stealing the formula for the spray. However, Lindsay tweeted: 'No formula was stolen for Sevin Nyne. It's a woman looking for a payday. That's it.'

Lindsay also had the upcoming release of *Labor Pains* on the horizon. In March, it had been announced that the film would not be released in cinemas, and instead it was to be shown on the ABC Family channel on 19 July 2009, and on DVD following that. The reviews for the movie weren't great, unfortunately, with the *LA Times* saying the movie was 'arduous' to watch, while Filmcritic.com said: 'It's not really the talent that's to blame in this movie – it's the material itself.' However, it was a hit on cable TV – it was the top-viewed cable movie among women the week it was broadcast, and over two million people tuned in to watch it.

Of course, for Lindsay, every piece of good news was followed by something bad. In August, her home was burgled, and when the burglars were caught in 2010, it turned out she was the latest victim of a gang of thieves the media dubbed The Bling Ring. The gang were a group of teenagers from an affluent neighbourhood in Los Angeles, who spent much of 2009 robbing the rich and famous. Among their victims were Paris Hilton, Orlando Bloom, Megan Fox and *The O.C.*'s Rachel Bilson. The idea was to steal jewels and clothes, and they amassed items worth over $3 million during their crime spree. On 23 August, they turned their attention to Lindsay's house, taking over $130,000 worth of clothes and jewellery. Lindsay allowed the police to release a video, taken from a surveillance camera at her house, that showed the robbers. Her video, along with one taken at *The Hills*' Audrina Partridge's home, gave the police proof that all the crimes were related, and it was not long before the gang were arrested for their involvement in the robberies.

If that wasn't enough, there was more bad news to come for Lindsay. She had been asked to join fashion label Ungaro as their artistic advisor in September, and on 4 October her first collection for the house was revealed during Paris Fashion Week. While Lindsay's own fashion line, 6126, had been a success with critics and shoppers alike, her collaboration with Ungaro was not well received. Designed by Spanish designer Estrella Archs, the clothes got mixed reviews, with Style.com noting that Archs and Lindsay only had a month to work on the collection, and then commenting: 'The show opened on an up note, with a strapless fuchsia plissé minidress – two Ungaro signatures rolled into one – and Archs turned the house's polka dots into a charming enough heart print on colourful sequinned jackets. So far, not so bad . . . but it wasn't destined to last. This quickly devolved into a bad joke of a fashion show, one with questionable colour combinations, "bad 1980s" draped silk jackets and drop-crotch pants, old-fashioned and ill-judged fur stoles, and, yes, tasteless sequin pasties.'

Virginie Mouzat, fashion director of French newspaper *Le Figaro*, commented that Lindsay may not have been the best choice for the Ungaro job: 'When you look at her own style, for me, she is not really relevant, first, regarding fashion and second, regarding a couture house like Ungaro. Maybe she would be relevant for [high street store] Kookaï.'

As the winter of 2009 began, it might seem impossible but things went from bad to worse. The press continued to speculate about Lindsay's relationship with Samantha Ronson (were they back together? On again? Off again?), and then, to add to the gossip, on 4 October, Lindsay's dad Michael thought it would be a good idea to release tapes of phone conversations he had had with Lindsay and her mother Dina to the website RadarOnline. One tape featured Lindsay crying and saying: 'Mommy says that I'm worse than you were . . . she doesn't stand by me. No one cares about me. They don't, by the way. It's about how they feel, not how I feel. It's not about me. It's never been about me, unless I fight for it.'

Michael told RadarOnline he was releasing the tapes to prove that Lindsay was in a fragile state and needed help. He told the *Daily Mail*: 'I have been trying for a year to help Lindsay with her problems privately through Lindsay, her mom, her attorney Blair Berk and even her new attorney Shawn Holley and the courts. But when that didn't work, and the calls I was getting from Dina and Lindsay needed immediate attention, it was recommended to me to go public in order to put pressure on Lindsay. Now that Dina and Lindsay continue to lie and deny their problems, and even I am sorry I had to take this route, but I have tried and tried to help Linds, and I have been lied about long enough.'

He also released a tape, reportedly from 2008, in which he and ex-wife Dina are talking about a relationship Lindsay may have had with the late Heath Ledger. In the recording, Dina tells Michael that, 'I would drop her off and they were friends very, very close, OK?' And that she was worried when Lindsay was drinking that her daughter 'will do something like Heath Ledger did in a second without thinking'.

Heath Ledger, the actor best known for his roles in

10 Things I Hate About You, Brokeback Mountain (for which he was nominated for a Best Actor Academy Award) and as the Joker in *The Dark Knight* (which won him a posthumous Oscar for Best Supporting Actor), died tragically on 22 January 2008. He was just twenty-eight years old, and the father of young Matilda Rose, his daughter with actress Michelle Williams, when he died of an accidental drug overdose.

Lindsay was quick to comment on Michael's decision to publish the tapes, writing on Twitter: 'My father is such a loser, and those recordings are from years ago. To release personal things is foul enough, but to edit them. I used to think that he needed the book for dummies on learning how to be a father. He needs the book for dummies on how to be a man.'

It seemed the perfect time for Lindsay to get away from the media storm around her. In December an interesting and very worthy project came her way that took her to somewhere a world away from Hollywood. The BBC asked her to travel to India, for a documentary called *Lindsay Lohan's Indian Journey*, in which she would highlight the issues of human trafficking in the country, bringing the children's plight to a younger audience on the BBC3 channel.

In the documentary, Lindsay was visibly moved when she visited the Sanlaap centre in Kolkata, a refuge for girls and women who are victims of violence and trafficking, and she wrote on her Twitter page: 'Trafficking is a big issue here. I'm [here to do] what I can, and I will continue to do so as long as life when time permits it.'

Danny Cohen, the controller of BBC3, explained why Lindsay was offered the project. 'We have to think, as a channel, how we can open up issues surrounding environment, development and globalisation for a media-literate audience of teens and twentysomethings who'll quite happily switch off and go online if you don't keep their attention,' he told the *Radio Times*. 'Finding a celebrity who genuinely cares about the issue really helps pull in a crowd that wouldn't otherwise switch on. But you have to be careful. If you get a rent-a-celeb, this audience can spot it a mile off. I've turned down more celebrity-led documentaries than I've put on the channel.'

The documentary's director, Maninderpal Sahota, talked about working with Lindsay, too. 'The producer met Lindsay at a social event before the project started, and found this was a passion for her. It's clearly not comparable, but as a result of working in an adult world since she was ten, she feels childhood is precious, and when you lose one you can never replace those years.'

Sahota also talked about Lindsay's behaviour during the trip. 'She behaved perfectly throughout – she slept in the same hotels, travelled in the same cars, just asked the right questions and clearly empathised with the children in a way hardened reporters might struggle to have done. Most people in rural villages in India have absolutely no idea who Lindsay Lohan is . . . When we finished, we had to race to the airport chased by paparazzi. That's not the kind of thing you get if you work with [BBC journalist and newsreader] Michael Buerk.'

Lindsay spoke to *Us Weekly* about the life-changing trip after her return. 'Making this documentary for BBC3 has allowed me to lend my voice to the real hardship faced by children who are trafficked. The strength of the young boys and girls I met has been truly humbling, and I hope my presence in India will bring awareness to the really important issues raised in making this film.'

She returned from India on 13 December, with Dina Lohan telling *People*: 'Lindsay is home from India now. I am so proud of her for going.' Lindsay, meanwhile, chatted about her journey on Twitter, saying the visit to India was 'the most amazing time of my life', she wrote. 'Focusing on celebrities and lies is so disconcerting, when we can be changing the world one child at a time . . . hope everyone can see that.'

Chapter Eleven
Ups and Downs

After she returned from India, Lindsay kept herself busy. First on the agenda was another charitable effort, following the devastating earthquake that hit the island of Haiti on 12 January 2010. An earthquake of 7.0 magnitude had struck in the afternoon, with its epicentre near the town of Legoane, sixteen miles west of the island's capital, Port-au-Prince. By 24 January there had been over fifty aftershocks, and it was estimated over three million people had been affected, with more than a million made homeless, and somewhere between 100,000 and 300,000 people killed.

Many countries offered humanitarian aid to the Haitians, and individual people rushed to help with donations to charities involved in the earthquake rescue, including UNICEF and Save the Children. Movie star George Clooney organised a telethon – *Hope for Haiti Now* – a global benefit aiming to raise money for charities working in Haiti, including the Red Cross, UNICEF, Oxfam America and The Clinton Bush Haiti Fund.

Lindsay also wanted to help. She began by donating some of the profits from her 6126 fashion line to the Haitian charities, and then on 16 February she worked with nightclub Altitude 360 in London to raise money at the iRock4Haiti fundraiser, held after London's Brit music awards, which raised much-needed money for the British Red Cross, followed by an auction on eBay. 'I am coming to London to host a party at Altitude London,' she said in a video to her fans. 'We are doing this in aid of Haiti, and I want you to help us raise as much money as possible. All the money we raise will go directly to the Red Cross. I hope to see you there.'

The charity's director, Mark Astarita, commented at the time: 'A big thank you to Lindsay Lohan and Altitude London for raising so much money at the iRock-4Haiti fundraiser, and now arranging such fabulous eBay auction prizes. All the money raised will be used by the British Red Cross to fund work in Haiti. Red Cross staff and volunteers have been in Haiti since the earthquake struck, and are committed to being there long term. There are many, many people in Haiti who still need help, so bid for one or more of these prizes today and help raise crucially needed funds.'

The auction included an NYPD car, used in a recent photo shoot with Lindsay, a day return trip to Paris in an Embraer Phenom 100 jet and a private party for two hundred people at the River Room in London. There was also an extra-special lot at the auction – fans could bid to spend the day with Lindsay in Los Angeles shopping and eating as part of a prize that also included first-class flights and four nights at the Peninsula Hotel in Beverly Hills.

While she was in London, Lindsay gave an exclusive interview with the *Sun* newspaper's Emma Cox, talking about her life. She told Cox how many of her problems with drink and drugs stemmed from her father talking to the press about her in 2007. 'When my father was going public, that's when I hit rock bottom,' she said. 'I abused substances too much, and it wasn't the answer to my problems. People need to know that. Now I'm in a place where I don't need to use anything and I can feel emotions because I choose to.'

'I learned from my mistakes,' she continued, 'and now I'm healthy and happier. I never want to be close to losing everything I worked for and aspired to have my whole life. Mind-altering substances are so dangerous. If I can teach others, especially teens, by sharing my experiences, then that's what I will continue to do. I've made some dreadful mistakes, but learned from them – that has probably saved my life.'

She also visited the British TV chat show *Alan Carr: Chatty Man* as a guest. Carr, a stand-up comedian, is known for his fun approach to interviews, and he often gets his subjects to reveal more than they intended. On 10 March, it was Lindsay's turn in the hot seat. As usual, Carr had fun with his guest, chatting about Lindsay's tattoos (she has two quotes from Marilyn Monroe on her arm: 'Stars, all we ask for is our right to twinkle' and 'I restore myself when I'm alone') and asking Lindsay such designed-to-shock questions as, 'Are you Arthur or are you Martha', and 'Are you back on the cock' – trying to get her to reveal her sexuality – which Lindsay took in good humour (jokingly calling Carr 'you bastard!') but she refused to answer.

Her appearance was praised by *Heatworld* for being 'very funny stuff', and it was truly hilarious to watch as she kept her dignity without spoiling Carr's fun (at the end of the interview, she told Carr he was a very funny man).

Shortly after Lindsay returned to LA following the *Chatty Man* interview, it was announced she had a new movie project. She was to be cast in the role of Linda Lovelace, one of two competing movies to be made about the actress. At first there was confusion as to which movie Lindsay had been cast in, until director Rob Epstein said that the announcement was 'definitely not true for our project, which is Lovelace'. Instead, Lindsay was to appear in the rival production, entitled *Inferno*, to be directed by Matthew Wilder.

Linda Lovelace's life was a controversial subject for a movie. Born Linda Boreman in 1949, she became involved with pimp Chuck Traynor at the age of twenty, and confessed that she worked as a prostitute for him until 1972. She also filmed hardcore pornographic 'loops' (illegal short sex films), and eventually a full-length porn movie was written especially for her – a script that would become the infamous *Deep Throat*. The movie, which was even reviewed in the *New York Times*, made her a star – she appeared on chat shows and the cover of *Esquire* magazine – and she went on to make a sequel before deciding never to make another porn movie. By 1980, she was married with children and had also become a born-again Christian. In interviews, she revealed that she had been coerced into making porn (with a gun held to her head), and she became a figurehead against porn in the last years of her life, alongside Andrea Dworkin, Gloria Steinem and Women Against Pornography. On 3 April 2002, she suffered massive internal injuries from a car accident, and she died on 22 April that year at the age of fifty-three.

Lindsay travelled to the Cannes Film Festival to promote her upcoming involvement in the movie. Unfortunately, on 16 October 2009, a judge had increased the length of time Lindsay would be on probation for her 2007 driving charges after it emerged she had not attended all the substance abuse meetings she should have. Her three-year probation, which would have expired before the Cannes trip in May 2010, was extended to four years so she could complete the programme. The trip to Cannes meant she was not in Los Angeles for the alcohol programme meetings she had to attend each week as part of her sentence, and a judge in Los Angeles issued a bench warrant – meaning Lindsay had to turn herself in when she arrived back in the US, or she would be arrested – for violating parole. Lindsay's lawyers paid her bail, so the warrant was then cancelled.

'She has a history of not keeping scheduled appointments,' said Judge Marsha Revel in a statement to the press when the warrant was issued. 'I couldn't be more clear about the priority of this case and getting things done. She should have made sure she either didn't go to Cannes or, if she went there, she should be back two days early. If she wanted to be here, it looks to the court she could have been here . . . She's not here. There's really no valid excuse.'

Lohan's attorney, Shawn Chapman Holley, said Lindsay had been delayed leaving Cannes because her passport had been stolen, and added that Lindsay now had it and would fly home as soon as she could get a flight. 'She had every intention to go to the alcohol programme yesterday,' Holley said. 'She had every intention of making it to court.'

'I'd like to see the ticket that she purchased,' said Deputy DA Danette Meyers to the press. 'I'd like to see some good-faith evidence that she was going to be here.'

The hearing to charge Lindsay for missing a court date while in Cannes was scheduled for 26 May, allowing her time to get back to the US. She arrived in court in a dark-grey trouser suit and listened as Judge Revel spoke of her decision to issue Lindsay with a SCRAM bracelet and strict probationary rules. Lindsay would be required to submit to drug and alcohol testing in Los Angeles every week, as well as attend an alcohol education programme. There would also be another hearing on 6 July regarding her probation, where Judge Revel would decide whether the alcohol-monitoring bracelet could be removed.

On 10 June, *Inferno* director Matthew Wilder talked to E! Entertainment News about his faith in Lindsay as an actress despite her recent troubles. 'It really breaks my heart,' he said. 'Every day I look and see these horrible things, and people wishing horrible things on her. The real person is very thoughtful, and cares about acting and has a lot of heart. Not this kind of screwball that's depicted every day in the press. They want a person to project what they hate or what they envy on. In a way I kind of want this murmuring of meanness right now,' Wilder added. 'I feel like when [*Inferno*] actually comes out, and when you see what the movie is and what she's doing, it's going to be so unexpected that it's going to actually kind of blow people's minds.'

Despite all her legal troubles, Lindsay was excited by the role. 'I'm playing Linda Lovelace, who was the first globally recognised porn star,' Lohan told journalist

Gaynor Flynn in an interview on 21 June with the *Sydney Morning Herald*. 'She became famous in the 1970s with her movie *Deep Throat*. We follow her through her ups and downs and show what really went on in her life.'

Flynn asked Lindsay whether she was bothered by the fact she would be making a movie about a woman who made porn. 'The way that Matthew [Wilder, the director] wants to shoot it, is not vulgar. It's not about the raw sex and the shots of her fully nude. It's more about getting into her psyche and seeing how scared she was. That's what I want to show most in the film.'

'She was just this lost girl, and she experienced things that you wouldn't ever wish on anyone,' Lindsay added. 'I think attractive women have a lot of insecurities that people don't necessarily see. I've been subjected to that kind of thing, too, and my mum: it reminds me of her relationship with my father. It's the story of someone who found herself when it was too late. It's a lesson to learn to be wise and not jump into things too fast.'

Two weeks after the interview, Lindsay was due back in court. It was 6 July, just four days after her twenty-fourth birthday. Judge Martha Revel noted that Lindsay had missed too many of the alcohol rehabilitation classes she had been ordered to attend following her two driving-under-the-influence offences, which meant Lindsay had indeed violated her probation.

Lindsay spoke to the court, saying: 'I'm not taking this as a joke. This is my life. It is my career. It is something I have worked for all my life. I don't want you to think I don't respect you and your terms, because I really did think that I was doing what I was supposed to do and I mean that with all my heart.'

Judge Revel handed down Lindsay's sentence: ninety days in jail and a ninety-day substance abuse programme after that, saying the actress was guilty of violating probation. Lindsay looked stunned before tears started rolling down her face. It was a scene played out around the world, as cameras were present in the court. Unfortunately, one of those cameras saw something other than just a distraught Lindsay crying. A close-up of one photo of Lindsay revealed she had the phrase 'Fuck U' written on one of her fingernails.

She later went on Twitter to explain the badly advised marking. 'Didn't we do our nails as a joke with our friend? It had nothing to do w/court. It's an air-bush design from a stencil xx.' Nonetheless, you would have thought she or her lawyer would have been sensible enough to wipe it off before appearing in court.

Lindsay was due to serve her sentence at the Century Regional Detention Facility in Lynwood, Los Angeles, starting on 20 July. It was the same place she had served her eighty-four-minute sentence in 2007. The *Daily Mail* reported that it was likely she would be placed in a special segregated cell for celebrities, and 'during her time behind bars, she will spend twenty-three hours a day in a two-bunk cell with a toilet and sink, and will be given an hour a day to shower, watch television, exercise outside and make phone calls.'

Despite being estranged from his daughter, Lindsay's father Michael was in court, along with her sister Ali. He later gave an interview to *Larry King Live* on CNN, talking about his reaction to the day's events. 'I feel dismay, but at the same time a little satisfaction that she's going to rehab. But the last thing in the world I wanted was for my daughter to go to jail.'

On 9 July, Lindsay responded on Twitter to her father's interviews following her court appearance. 'I love my mother . . . she is amazing and strong, she's all I could ask for and more, by taking on the role of my mother and father all my life.'

Before she was to begin her sentence, Lindsay still had some work commitments – and the first was to shoot a cover and give an interview to men's magazine *Maxim*. Conducted just a week before she was due to go to jail, the shoot featured Lindsay in a black and white striped bikini, looking healthy (though it was commented on that the swimsuit resembled prison stripes!) and the interview, for the September 2010 issue, featured Lindsay chatting about her life. 'I am feeling strong,' she said, of her future. 'I've experienced a lot in my life, and my mom has given me a lot of faith. This too shall pass.'

Maxim asked her what her motto for life was. 'Stay true to yourself always,' she replied. 'At the end of the day, you have to look at yourself in the mirror and be content with the choices you've made, and will make, in your life.'

Lindsay also agreed to do a photo shoot and interview with *Vanity Fair* magazine before she went to prison (the cover shoot and feature appeared in the magazine's October issue, on sale after she was released). The photos, of Lindsay looking like a classic Hollywood goddess aboard the *Sovereign*, a boat built for Judy Garland in 1961, were stunning. And the interview was revealing.

She spoke about her shock at her sentence ('I was just thrown. I was under the assumption that it was going to be a progress-report-type hearing. I had no idea that it was going to be anything like a trial') and how her troubles had become headline news around the world (being interviewed on TV show *The View*, even President Barack Obama said he was 'aware of her predicament').

'I don't care what anyone says,' she told *Vanity Fair* reporter Nancy Jo Sales. 'I know that I'm a damn good actress, and it's been my passion since I was a child, and I know that when I care about something I put a hundred per cent and more into it. And I know that in my past I was young and irresponsible – but that's what growing up is. You learn from your mistakes. I'm not getting any younger. I want my career back. I want the respect that I had when I was doing great movies. And if that takes not going out to a club at night, then so be it. It's not fun anyway.'

Lindsay talked about how she had got to this point, facing jail time. 'I didn't have any structure,' she said of moving to LA as a teen. 'I lost all the structure in my life. I think a lot of it was because, when I was doing my first slew of movies, it was very go, go, go and I had a lot of responsibility . . . I was eighteen, nineteen with a ton of money and no one really here to tell me that I couldn't do certain things . . . And I see where that's gotten me now. And I don't like it.'

Sales also asked Lindsay how she felt about her father talking to the press after her arrest on 6 July. 'I feel sorry for him. Obviously, it shows a cry for attention in so many ways. He's not happy with himself. Therefore, he has to project it onto others. The worst part of it is, you turn around and you see your dad crying and normally you'd be, like, happy that your father's there. But then he has to go and do an interview right after.' She added that she hadn't wanted him at the court, and didn't want him near her younger sister Ali. 'That moment where I turned and she was crying – it was heartbreaking.'

The cameras were once again ready to focus on Lindsay and her family on 20 July when Lindsay appeared in court before being taken to jail. She was handcuffed, and the judge ordered no cameras could take photos of her once she was taken into custody. According to the Associated Press, she was taken in an unmarked Sheriff's Department car to the Lynwood facility, and it was announced she was most likely to serve around thirteen days of her ninety-day sentence due to prison overcrowding.

She was released from jail on 2 August 2010, as expected. Sheriff's Department spokesman Steve Whitmore told the press that Lindsay was discharged at 1.20 a.m. on Monday 2 August, and taken directly to an inpatient rehabilitation centre at Ronald Reagan UCLA Medical Center to complete the rehab phase of her sentence.

While Lindsay was in rehab, Michael Lohan decided to talk to the press again. In an interview with *Fabulous*, he said that Lindsay's problems began when he and Dina split up. 'When her mother, Dina, and I broke up in 2005 it all fell apart for Lindsay,' he said. 'Lindsay was in so much pain. She was subjected to making decisions over who she should trust, her mom or her dad. It tore Lindsay up inside. When she had her family together, she had it all together. When she didn't have her family, it all fell apart.' He blamed his ex-wife for some of Lindsay's problems. 'Dina was living vicariously through Lindsay. Lindsay ended up around all the wrong people, and they were there for all the wrong reasons. It was like she didn't know who to trust any more. All I care about is Lindsay having her life back. It's what any child of divorce needs. Lindsay needs to be off drugs and to have both her parents there for her.'

Meanwhile, Lindsay's mother gave an interview to journalist Matt Lauer on the US TV programme *The Today Show*. In the interview, Dina talked about the court case, saying: 'I think the judge went overboard and played serious hardball with Lindsay,' and 'I'm not condoning drinking and driving, but she's still paying the price for what she did in 2007.' She also mentioned she had visited Lindsay in jail ('I visited her behind glass') and, when Lauer asked how Lindsay was coping, Dina replied: 'She's been through a lot. Lindsay was in with alleged murderers, and she's become friends with a lot of them! She has rolled with the punches and she's doing wonderfully.'

One other thing Dina mentioned in the interview was the intense media scrutiny Lindsay was under. 'She has a lot of media surrounding her. We can't go out without about twelve cars following us. It's a little bizarre. In the old days, people like Julia Roberts and those girls didn't really have people following them and their relationships. It wasn't as magnified as now. With the internet, it's become so much more profound.'

She was quite right. Now everyone has a camera phone to snap shots of any celebrities they see, and the Internet means it can be made available around the world instantly. In an interview with *Rolling Stone*, Leonardo DiCaprio noted how different things had been for him as a famous teen who grew up in the spotlight just a few years before Lindsay. 'I got to be wild and nuts, and I didn't suffer as much as people do now, where they have to play it so safe that they ruin their credibility. I didn't care what anyone thought.'

Unfortunately, Lindsay became an adult at a time when websites such as TMZ.com prints every piece of gossip and every photo on every celebrity you can think of.

The gossip websites were, of course, the first to print the news that Lindsay had left rehab on 24 August, which meant she had done considerably fewer than the ninety days of rehabilitation the judge had sentenced her to. Her lawyer, Shawn Chapman Holley, told the press that the reason for Lindsay's early release was 'because the treating doctors at UCLA felt she had done everything required of her there'.

There were some conditions to her release. The *Washington Post* reported that Lindsay would have to undergo a strict outpatient rehab programme and frequent counselling; she would have to submit to frequent alcohol and drug testing, and also continue to live in Los Angeles where she could be monitored. In court (which Lindsay did not attend), the judge who made these stipulations, Elden S. Fox, dismissed the two drugs charges from her 2007 arrests, and also said Lindsay would be taken off supervised probation once she had complied with all his orders.

Lindsay couldn't retreat completely out of the spotlight, however. In August of 2009 she had filmed a small role in a new movie, *Machete*, and it was due for release on 10 September 2010. While Lindsay declined to appear at the movie's première, the press was eager to see what her most recent movie role was all about.

The character of Machete Cortez, who is at the heart of the movie, was actually created for the family movie *Spy Kids* by director Robert Rodriguez. Then, in 2007, Rodriguez and Quentin Tarantino made a homage to B-movies called *Grindhouse*, which featured trailers for fake movies at the beginning of the film. One of those fake trailers was for *Machete*, and Rodriguez liked the idea so much he decided to make the movie itself with the help of co-director Ethan Maniquis.

The enjoyably tacky film opens as Machete Cortez (Danny Trejo), a Mexican *federale*, tries to rescue a kidnapped girl. Unfortunately, he crosses both his corrupt boss and a drug lord (Steven Seagal), who kills Machete's family and leaves him for dead. Three years later, he is down on his luck and is coerced by businessman Booth (Jeff Fahey) into accepting a murder contract to kill a corrupt US state senator (Robert De Niro). He is then set up by Booth, and ends up on the run from just about everybody including a government agent (Jessica Alba). Wanting revenge, Machete kidnaps Booth's wife and daughter April (Lindsay Lohan) – getting them to appear in an amateur sex movie before stashing them in a church – and the action goes into fifth gear when all the good and bad guys turn up, bullets start flying, and April appears in a nun's habit ready to shoot anyone in her way.

Before the movie started filming, Robert Rodriguez had told the audience at movie festival Comic-Con that he really wanted Lindsay in the movie. 'Lindsay's cool. There's actually a cool part in the movie for her if she takes it.'

'April was born into a life of privilege and takes everything she has for granted,' said Lindsay in a press interview for the movie. 'But she undergoes a big change. As an actress, I like pushing the envelope.'

The movie was released to favourable reviews. Nigel Floyd of *Time Out* magazine called it a 'gleefully excessive pastiche of an exploitation picture', and Frank Scheck of *The Hollywood Reporter* said it 'delivers everything that was promised [by the original fake trailer]'.

It was great that Lindsay was part of something that was getting positive press. However, less than two weeks later, on 20 September, sadly she was in the news for the wrong reasons again. It turned out that she had failed one of her court-ordered drug tests. She posted messages to her fans on Twitter, saying: 'Regrettably, I did in fact fail my most recent drug test and if I am asked, I am prepared to appear before Judge Fox next week as a result. Substance abuse is a disease, which unfortunately doesn't go away overnight. I am working hard to overcome it and am taking positive steps. This was certainly a setback for me, but I am taking responsibility for my actions and I'm prepared to face the consequences.'

Judge Elden Fox had told Lindsay that if she failed any of her drug tests, she could face thirty days in jail. CNN reported on 24 September that 'Judge Elden Fox ordered the preliminary revocation of Lohan's probation Friday morning based on a probation report saying she tested positive for controlled-substance use. The probation revocation hearing was set for 22 October.' This meant that, because she had failed the drug test, Lindsay was due to go straight to jail until 22 October. She was taken away in handcuffs, but a second court hearing was then held later in the day in which Judge Patricia Schnegg granted Lindsay bail at a cost of $300,000. She ordered that Lindsay also had to wear a SCRAM bracelet and appear before the court again in a month, where the judge would decide what punishment she would receive for failing the drug test. Lindsay emerged from jail after spending fourteen hours there.

While Lindsay was accompanied to court by her mother Dina, her father Michael sat at the back of the court away from the family and then emerged to give an interview to CNN on the courthouse steps. 'I pray to God that Shawn [Chapman Holley, Lindsay's lawyer] does the right thing and advises her to go right into rehab now, and show the judge she's serious, because in thirty days when she goes back before the judge he can do whatever he wants,' he said. 'I just hope the judge remands Lindsay to a rehab for a longer period of time, and that the people in Lindsay's life that are destroying her and leading her down the wrong path are weeded out.'

Three days after the court case, Lindsay checked herself into the Betty Ford Center in Rancho Mirage,

California. The famous clinic was established by Betty Ford, the wife of former President Gerald Ford, and businessman Leonard Firestone. Betty had battled her own addictions to alcohol and painkillers, and it had been her goal to set up a special treatment centre for the needs of women.

On 22 October, Lindsay's lawyer returned to court to hear the judge's ruling. It was decided that she should remain in rehab at the Betty Ford Center until 3 January for the violation of her probation (failing the drug test). According to the Betty Ford Center website, the centre provides treatment for those whose 'life under the influence of alcohol and/or drugs has become unmanageable'. The in-patient programme, which costs just under $30,000 for thirty days, includes a clinical and medical assessment, detoxification and treatment services. Each patient lives in a hotel-like room (complete with patio) in one of the single-sex resident halls set on the twenty-acre campus, and is assigned a treatment team of a physician, nurse, psychologist, counsellor, dietician, fitness trainer and chemical dependency advisor.

It sounded the perfect retreat for Lindsay to finally get herself well again. However, even inside Betty Ford, she made headlines again in December when an employee of the Centre accused Lindsay of battery. Dawn Holland told police she had been hit by Lindsay while trying to get her to submit to a drug and alcohol test, but after an investigation, police decided against filing a battery charge against Lindsay with District Attorney's Office spokesman John Hall telling Reuters reporters on 30 March 2011 that there was insufficient evidence to charge Lindsay with the crime. Holland, meanwhile, left the Betty Ford Center's employment days after the incident. In a statement, the Betty Ford Center explained why: 'Regrettably, on 21 December 2010, one of our employees violated strict confidentiality guidelines and laws by publicly identifying patients in a media interview and by disclosing a privileged document. The employee has been terminated by the Betty Ford Center.'

Due to her stay in rehab, Lindsay's role in *Inferno*, the Linda Lovelace movie, was finally cancelled before the end of 2010. In September, director Matthew Wilder told the press he was trying to accommodate Lindsay's legal problems by changing the shooting location of the movie ('We are going to shoot the movie in Los Angeles. We had looked around at various locations in Louisiana, but we want to do it here now. That way, if there is anything that needs to be dealt with here, we can do that here. We don't have to get a special pass to go from this time to that time, and it will all be in-town. So that's our plan for right now.') However, with Lindsay in rehab until January 2011, that plan was unworkable. In November, he spoke to E! Online. 'We have stuck by Lindsay very patiently for a long time with a lot of love and support. Ultimately, the impossibility of insuring her – and some other issues – have made it impossible for us to go forward.' Lindsay was no longer starring in the movie, and in the spring of 2011 it was announced that *Inferno: A Linda Lovelace Story* would start production soon with *Watchmen* actress Malin Akerman in the lead role instead.

As 2011 began, twenty-four-year-old Lindsay emerged from the Betty Ford Center to an uncertain future. She had sold her old West Hollywood apartment, ready to start afresh, as she had hinted on New Year's Day when she tweeted: 'Today's the first day of the rest of my life.' When she left rehab on 3 January, Lindsay moved into a new Venice Beach house in Los Angeles, next door to her ex-girlfriend Samantha Ronson's home, which she was renting for a reported $5,000 a month.

A source told UK's *Look* magazine that Samantha wasn't best pleased about her new neighbour. 'Samantha came home only to find Lindsay moving in next door. She was shaking her head and looking disgusted. She kept saying, "I didn't plan it this way."' Photographers taking photos of moving boxes being taken into Lindsay's new home asked Samantha if she had any New Year resolutions, to which, according to *Look*, she replied: 'No, I'm too pissed off right now.'

Lindsay had a beautiful home to settle into, regardless of the feelings of her next-door neighbour. The four-bedroom white house boasts four bathrooms, a stunning kitchen and a balconied area above the living room, as well as floor-to-ceiling windows to take in the coastal Venice Beach view. A district in the west side of Los Angeles, just south of Santa Monica, Venice is known for its promenade, beaches and the street performers, fortune-tellers and artists that line the boardwalk. It has always had a reputation for being one of the most vibrant and eclectic areas of Los Angeles, attracting artists and surfers and actors including Anna Paquin, Christian Bale, Tim Robbins, Robert Downey Jr and Nicolas Cage. Julia Roberts lived there for a decade, and it was legendary Doors frontman Jim Morrison's home for two years, around the time the band was formed. It's also been the setting for numerous movies including *LA Story*, *White Men Can't Jump*, *Falling Down* and *Speed* (and Venice High School doubled as Rydell High, the school in the movie *Grease*).

Venice also boasts an interesting collection of boutiques and shops. On 22 January 2011, Lindsay went into one, an upmarket jewellery shop called Kamofie & Co, and tried some jewellery on. Just over two weeks later, on 9 February, it was reported that she would be charged with felony grand theft for stealing a necklace worth $2,500 from the store that night. 'We vehemently deny these allegations and, if charges are filed, we will fight them in court, not in the press,' Lindsay's lawyer, Shawn Chapman Holley, said in a statement to the press when the news broke.

CNN reported that Lindsay had walked out of the store wearing the necklace and a statement from the district attorney's office said: 'The owner reported the theft to the Los Angeles Police Department, which investigated the allegation and presented evidence to the DA's office last week.' The necklace was handed in to police, but if Lindsay was found guilty of theft, she was facing up to three years in prison.

On 23 March, Lindsay's lawyers rejected a plea deal in which she would have received a reduced sentence by pleading guilty rather than going to court. It wasn't a clear-cut case, however. First, it emerged that the jewellery store owners had sold the rights to their security video – which showed Lindsay in the store on the day in question – to a website, and then it was discovered a representative for the store had spoken to a book agent about a possible book deal, according to CNN. Steve Sadow, a criminal defence attorney, talked to CNN about the implications this had for Lindsay's case. 'The pursuit of a book deal, coupled with the sale of the surveillance video, clearly demonstrates that the owner is interested in money and publicity, and has trumped up the allegations against Ms Lohan to further his own interests, not to seek justice.'

Lindsay had also told friends she was sure that she had been loaned the necklace when she left the store. 'Ms Lohan has maintained her innocence from the moment this case was filed and she has never wavered,' her lawyer said in a statement. 'Though many advised her to follow the safe route by taking "the deal", the truth is, Ms Lohan is innocent; she has a strong defence;

and we are confident that a jury will listen to the evidence fairly and acquit her.' A hearing was scheduled for 22 April, when the judge, Stephanie Sautner, would hear evidence and decide whether the case should go to trial, and also decide whether Lindsay had violated her probation by taking the necklace.

Lindsay appeared before the court on 22 April as witnesses testified as part of Deputy District Attorney Danette Meyers' case against Lindsay. Two of the witnesses were police officers on the case – including one to whom Lindsay's assistant had given the necklace and another who testified Lindsay had been photographed by the paparazzi wearing it – and the third was the jewellery store's owner, Sofia Kaman. She testified that Lindsay had tried on the necklace, and that ten minutes after she had left the store it was noticed that the necklace was missing. When asked if she had entered into an agreement for Lindsay to take the necklace and pay for it later, Kaman replied: 'No.' She also said she waited a day to report the theft because Lindsay had told her she would return the next day to buy a ring, but she never came back to the store. Lindsay's lawyer, Shawn Chapman Holley, then asked how Kaman didn't notice Lindsay still had the necklace round her neck when she left the store, even though it would have been clearly visible. 'I wasn't looking at her chest,' Kaman replied, 'I was looking at her face.'

According to Anthony McCartney of the Associated Press, Deputy DA Meyers told the court that 'we believe there was a clear abuse of discretion' on Lindsay's part when it came to the necklace, and Judge Sautner agreed, saying she thought Lindsay meant to take the piece of jewellery. 'I see intent here,' she told the court, 'I see a level of brazenness with "Let me see what I can get away with here."' Sautner decided, however, to reduce the charge against Lindsay from grand theft to a misdemeanour. 'I'm going to give her an opportunity,' she said of the decision.

Sautner then handed out Lindsay's sentence for violating her probation – 120 days in prison, and 500 hours of community service that would be spent at the Los Angeles County morgue and at a women's shelter. 'She'll be doing basic janitorial work, Coroner Assistant Chief Ed Winter told *People* about her community service at the morgue. 'She won't be handling any dead bodies, but she'll certainly see them.' Meanwhile, Lisa Watson, the CEO of the Downtown Women's Center, where Lindsay would fulfil the rest of her community service, told RadarOnline: 'The DWC is a life-changing experience for all who walk through our doors. DWC hopes that Miss Lohan is inspired by her experience here.'

Lindsay was led away from court, but released at 9 p.m. the same day after her $75,000 bail was paid. The next step was to appear for a pretrial hearing on 11 May, with the jewellery theft trial due to start on 3 June. The press speculated that Lindsay could be looking at some serious jail time, and rumours started to spread that she would now agree a plea deal to limit the amount of time she would serve in prison.

Days after her appearance in court, Lindsay made an unscheduled appearance on the *Tonight Show* with Jay Leno to talk about her current situation. Receiving a standing ovation when she appeared in front of the live studio audience, Lindsay looked calm in a black silk jumpsuit, her blond hair in a loose bun. 'I've made a lot of poor decisions, and I'm dealing with the consequences,' she told Leno. He asked her how she felt when she received a 120-day jail sentence on what was, ironically, Good Friday. 'I was kind of shocked, I didn't expect the outcome to be what it was,' she answered. 'But I'm a big girl, and I'm going to do what I'm told to do. I am taking responsibility.' Leno asked her if she thought she had been treated unfairly in court, but she replied: 'I think that I was treated the way I should have been treated.'

The Lindsay in front of the Leno audience was a calmer, more grown-up woman than tabloids had led people to believe she was. 'I'm not a kid any more,' she continued. 'I'm twenty-four, I've made a lot of mistakes and I recognise that. I feel like I've let a lot of my fans down by putting myself in situations when I was young and wasn't thinking clearly.

'I just want to be the person, and the actress, that I aspire to be, and be in this industry and make movies and do what I love to do, and bring characters to life that people can relate to. And my fans have been really supportive of me doing that.'

Leno told Lindsay that his recent chat-show guest Jane Fonda, who had appeared with Lindsay in *Georgia Rule*, had said that Lindsay was one of the best young actresses she had worked with. 'That's amazing, coming from her,' Lindsay replied. 'As long as I can stay focused, I can achieve what I want to achieve.'

She also spoke about her family, saying: 'My mom's amazing, she's really strong. My sister's here with me . . . I have good people in my life.' But Lindsay refused to talk about her father, among reports he had twice been seen outside Lindsay's home but not allowed in since her court date.

The interview was upbeat, warm and a perfect way for Lindsay to show the world that, despite everything, she was doing OK. Before the end of the interview, Jay Leno asked her where she hoped she would be when she turned thirty in six years' time, and he got a very positive reply: 'Hopefully sitting here, after winning an Oscar.'

And despite the uncertainty of her court case, by the end of April Lindsay had even signed up to her next movie, *Gotti: Three Generations*, which was due to film in September 2011. She was to play Kim Gotti, the daughter-in-law of John Gotti. Gotti, who died in 2002, was an American mobster who became head of the notorious Gambino crime family. Known as the 'Teflon Don' because criminal charges against him never seemed to stick, he nonetheless ended up in jail in 1992 for racketeering, conspiracy to commit murder, tax evasion and extortion. Once imprisoned, his son John Jr was sus-pected of taking over the crime family before he turned his life around and renounced crime in 2004. Gotti Jr sold the rights to his family's story to producer Marc Fiore, because, he told *Variety*: 'I'm most interested in this story getting told accurately, and I think Marc can do that. This is not going to be an exposé of the mob or a shoot-'em-up.'

The movie's director is Barry Levinson, who has made such acclaimed movies as *Rain Man*, *Good Morning, Vietnam* and *Diner*, while Lindsay's co-stars include John Travolta as John Gotti, his real-life wife Kelly Preston as Gotti's wife Victoria and, at the time of writ-ing, Al Pacino as underboss Neil Dellacroce. Joe Pesci will possibly star as Angelo Ruggiero, one of Gotti Sr's closest friends. Travolta, in an interview with *Us Magazine*, said he was excited to have Lindsay on board. 'I know whatever she would like to do [in the movie] would be great.' He jokingly added, 'I know, first hand, Lindsay happens to be a very big fan of mine from years ago when she was a little girl and liked [*Grease*'s] Danny Zuko and [*Welcome Back Kotter*'s] Vin-nie Barbarino, so I always thought she was gorgeous and talented and filled with a lot of depth!'

Steve Honig of Fiore Films spoke to the *Daily Mail* about the decision to cast Lindsay. 'She has been cast in this role. She still has the role, and we're very excited about her being in the movie. We're not going to spec-ulate on "What if this happens, what if that happens",' he said. 'We're dealing with a few unknowns. Once we start understanding exactly what the situation is, that's when we can start making some decisions.'

Luckily, for both Lindsay and the Gotti production, the court date on 11 May removed any uncertainty. Lindsay did not appear in court, but her lawyer negotiated a 'no contest' plea with regards to the jewellery theft, and she was ordered to hand herself over to begin a 120-day prison sentence by 17 June 2011. The judge, who also sentenced Lindsay to 480 hours' community service for the crime, released details of a probation report on Lindsay, which mentioned that she 'appears to be continuing to struggle with substance abuse issues', although Judge Sautner added to the court: 'I don't think the root of her problems is substance abuse. I think she has other problems for which she self-medicates.'

It was announced that Lindsay's sentence for the theft would run concurrently with the similar sentence she received in April for her probation violation.

A written statement from Lindsay was read out later that day to the press. 'I am glad to be able to put this past me and move on with my life and my career. I support the judge's decision, and hold myself accountable for being in this situation. I have already started my community service at the Downtown Women's Center, and thank everyone there for their warm welcome,' she also said. 'I hope to be able to fulfil my obligation without any press attention. I think the media spotlight should be on issues such as homelessness and domestic violence instead of on me.'

Los Angeles County Sheriff spokesman Steve Whitmore confirmed that it was very unlikely Lindsay would serve anything like 120 days in jail. 'Because of budget constraints, and because we're under a federal consent decree that requires us to curb our overcrowding situation, non-violent offenders, lesser crimes, get twenty per cent of their sentence,' he said, adding that it was more likely Lindsay would serve her time – possibly as little as sixteen days – under house arrest instead of in a jail cell.

Indeed, Lindsay served no jail time at all, instead spending thirty-five days under house arrest with an electronic ankle bracelet from 27 May until 29 June. It wasn't plain sailing – during the sentence she failed an alcohol test following a party at her home and was admonished by Judge Stephanie Sautner. 'Don't give people reason to hate you. Don't do stupid things that fly in the spirit of the court's order,' Sautner told Lindsay. 'You know I sentenced you to jail. You know I didn't sentence you to house arrest, and what do you do? You have barbecues at your house so your neighbours are writing letters about you.' Sautner went on to ban Lindsay from having more than one friend or relative over at her home at any one time for the remainder of the sentence.

Her release on 29 June allowed Lindsay to return to

community service and celebrate her twenty-fifth birthday on 2 July. However, by 19 October she was back in front of Judge Sautner for missing nine psychotherapy appointments and only completing twenty-one out of 360 hours of community service at the Downtown Women's Center. She was once again sentenced to spend time in jail, and on 7 November served five hours of a thirty-day prison sentence for violating her probation agreement. She was also told she had to spend 423 hours at the county morgue, where she had been cleaning floors and washing sheets for the previous two weeks.

It seemed Lindsay's legal woes were never-ending. However, just as she emerged from jail it was announced that she did have a new project on the horizon – Lindsay had agreed to pose in *Playboy* magazine's January issue for a rumoured $1 million. Her manager, Steve Honig, told reporters that 'the pictorial is absolutely fantastic and very tasteful, and will be accompanied by an interview that will let readers see another side of Lindsay'.

Playboy founder Hugh Hefner, meanwhile, revealed: 'It's a classic tribute inspired by the original Tom Kelly nude pictorial of Marilyn Monroe, a portion of which was the original playmate in the very first issue of *Playboy*'

When the magazine went on sale at the end of December 2011, it was a huge hit, with Hefner tweeting that the tasteful shoot was 'breaking sales records'. Perhaps

it was a sign that as 2011 became 2012 things were looking up for the actress. Certainly, as 2012 began, more
positive stories about her started to appear in the news.
She was tipped to win the lead role in a TV movie
based on the romance between Elizabeth Taylor and
Richard Burton, and she also signed to be the face of
Jag Jeans.

'As Jag Jeans' newest endorser, Lindsay embodies
the strength and fearlessness of the woman of today.
She is unafraid to be who she is. She is fierce yet exudes
feminine grace,' a spokesman for Jag Jeans commented. 'Lindsay was so involved with the shoot that
she would go as far as adjusting items on the set. She
even requested scissors so she could personally fray
the edges of her black crêpe blouse because she
believed it would look better that way. Lindsay would
take a hands-on approach to her shots, was more than
willing to change her hairstyle mid-shoot and even
used her own personal jewelry and accessories when
needed.'

Praise indeed. And on 17 January 2012 she received
a glowing progress report concerning her ongoing
probation. 'Just keep doing what you're doing, you
appear to be doing it well,' Judge Sautner told Lindsay. 'The probation officer has written a favourable
report, as has the volunteer centre.'

Following the traumas of the past few years, perhaps a wiser, calmer Lindsay is emerging, one who will
fulfil the amazing promise she showed in such movies

as *The Parent Trap*, *Freaky Friday* and *Mean Girls* before she was even an adult. An extremely talented actress with a gift for comedy, a memorable voice and a bright-as-sunshine smile, she deserves to be known once more for her talent rather than for her personal life.

'People really have come to believe that I started in this because I wanted to be a celebrity,' she told *Interview* in 2008. 'But that was never my intention.'

'I wanted to be a movie star. But movie stars are not what they used to be.'

Lindsay Lohan Timeline

December 1984: Michael Lohan and Donata 'Dina' Sullivan meet in Bloomingdale's in Manhattan and start dating.

2 November 1985: Michael and Dina marry.

2 July 1986: Lindsay Dee Lohan is born in New York to parents Michael and Dina.

1987: Michael Jr is born. The family now live in the town of Cold Spring Harbor in New York State.

1989: Lindsay, aged three, is signed to the Ford Modeling Agency. 'She was reputedly the first redhead that Ford had ever hired,' said Michael Fleeman of *People*. 'And she was only three years old. So before she could barely even speak entire sentences, she was in show business.' Lindsay went on to appear in adverts for Toys R Us, Sears, Burger King and Abercrombie Kids, among others.

1990: Michael is sent to Nassau County Jail on charges of fraud. He was sentenced to thirty-seven months in prison followed by five years' probation, and also received a $200,000 fine. Dina relocates the family to her home town of Merrick.

1993: Michael is released from prison.

22 December 1993: Michael and Dina have another daughter, Aliana (known as Ali).

1996: Lindsay wins the role of Alli Fowler in the long-running daytime soap *Another World*. She stays in the soap for a year.

At this time, Disney is searching for a young actress to appear in their updated version of *The Parent Trap*, which originally starred Hayley Mills. Lindsay is one of hundreds of girls who audition. 'I saw Lindsay on a tape made in New York and thought she was just electric,' said director Nancy Meyers.

16 June 1996: Dina and Michael have a fourth child, Dakota, also known as Cody.

1997: Lindsay wins the role of twins Hallie and Annie ('I started jumping up and down on the bed in my hotel room and I called all my friends. It was so exciting because I never thought that day would come,' she said of winning the part) and films the movie alongside veteran actors Dennis Quaid and Natasha Richardson.

Dad Michael breaks the terms of his probation and visits Lindsay on set. He is sentenced to a further year in prison.

31 July 1998: *The Parent Trap* is released in cinemas in the US, and receives rave reviews for Lindsay's performance. *Entertainment Weekly* said: 'Responsibility for making this Trap tender rests heaviest on the bird-size shoulders of auburn-haired, freckle-faced Lohan, now eleven, who won the unenviable job of making us forget about Hayley Mills – at least temporarily. The natural, pleasurable 1990s hipness this newcomer brings to her assignment is therefore all the more impressive.'

1998: Lindsay signs a three-movie deal with Disney, but takes a break from film-making to concentrate on her schooling.

6 March 1999: Lindsay wins the award for Best Performance In A Feature Film By A Leading Young Actress for her roles in *The Parent Trap* at the Youth In Film Awards, held in Studio City, California.

October 1999: Filming begins on the Disney TV movie *Life-Size*, in which Lindsay co-stars alongside model and actress Tyra Banks.

Early 2000: Lindsay films the pilot episode of the sitcom *Bette* in New York, appearing as Bette Midler's daughter Rose. Filming for the actual series is then relocated to Los Angeles, but because Lindsay does not want to leave her school, she resigns from the role.

May 2001: Filming begins on Lindsay's second TV movie for Disney, *Get A Clue*, in Toronto and New York.

January 2002: Lindsay starts dating pop singer Aaron Carter, causing a feud between her and Carter's ex-girlfriend, TV star Hilary Duff.

2002: She signs on for the lead role in a remake of Disney's *Freaky Friday*, alongside Jamie Lee Curtis. The part also featured Lindsay's first onscreen kiss, with actor Chad Michael Murray. 'I was so nervous because it's kissing someone I don't know extremely well who's a good-looking, twenty-one-year-old guy, and you have to do it in front of a hundred people on the set,' she said at the time.

Lindsay contributes a song to the movie's soundtrack; she also signs a recording contract with Estefan Enterprises, run by Emilio Estefan.

Early 2003: Lindsay begins filming *Confessions of a Teenage Drama Queen* in Canada.

Late 2003: Lindsay films the teen comedy *Mean Girls*, written by Tina Fey of *Saturday Night Live* fame.

February 2004: Lindsay moves into an apartment with fellow actress Raven-Symone. 'We met at the *Vanity Fair* photo shoot and she mentioned she wanted an apartment and I said I did, too,' Lindsay told *Girls' Life*.

14 February 2004: *Confessions of a Teenage Drama Queen* is released in the US, but does not do well at the box office or receive good reviews.

30 April 2004: *Mean Girls* is released in the US to rave reviews and big box office. It was later crowned one of the best movies of the decade by *Entertainment Weekly*. 'Right now, she's the reigning teen queen,' Rob Friedman, vice-chairman of Paramount Pictures, told the *Observer* about Lindsay. '*Mean Girls* struck a chord with moviegoers. It's something that not only young girls can identify with but also older women and men. Lindsay is identifiable. She's not an unreal personality. Audiences can relate to her.'

Following her appearance in the movie, the press speculates that Lindsay has had breast implants. 'I'm seventeen years old, my mother would never let me. I'd be deathly afraid, and it's unnecessary . . . but I'm glad people think I have a nice chest,' Lindsay said at the time.

1 May 2004: Lindsay presents *Saturday Night Live* in New York, the iconic live comedy show.

4 June 2004: Michael Lohan is accused of assaulting his brother-in-law Matt Sullivan at a family party on 23 May, and arrested.

5 June 2004: Lindsay is the youngest-ever host of the *MTV Movie Awards* in Los Angeles. 'I'm nervous, I have butterflies, but it's a great experience. It's a big adrenaline rush,' she told MTV News at the time.

29 June 2004: Michael Lohan is arrested for leaving a hotel without paying a $3,000 room bill. He is asked to appear in court to answer the charges on 26 August.

2 July 2004: Lindsay celebrates her eighteenth birthday and goes public with her romance with *That 70s Show* star Wilmer Valderrama. 'We've become really, really good friends. I love him to death. He's a great guy. He's been there for me with all this family shit going on. We'll see what happens. If this matures into a serious relationship, he'll be my first real boyfriend. But I don't know – I'm only eighteen. I wanna have fun,' she told *Rolling Stone* at the time.

July 2004: Lindsay signs with Casablanca Records and starts work on her first album. Kara DioGuardi (who has written for Britney Spears and Christina Aguilera and was a judge on *American Idol*), John Shanks (Take That, Sting), Cory Rooney (Destiny's Child, Jennifer Lopez) and TJ and Taryll Jackson (sons of Tito Jackson of the Jackson Five) are among the writers and producers working with her.

Summer 2004: Michael and Dina Lohan separate.

August 2004: Lindsay begins filming *Herbie: Fully Loaded* for Disney and also records her first album, *Speak*. 'I had to leave the house at four in the morning to go on set. I would literally get home at two in the morning, sleep, then sleep in the car for an hour. I leave the set, so tired from the day, then be in the studio until, like, 2.30 in the morning,' she said of her busy schedule.

3 August 2004: Lindsay has a minor car accident in Los Angeles.

8 August 2004: Having been nominated for six awards, Lindsay wins four – Choice Hissy Fit, Choice Actress, Choice Blush and Choice Breakout Movie Star – at the Teen Choice Awards.

October 2004: Michael is again arrested, this time for allegedly assaulting a sanitation worker in New York.

Lindsay films a cameo performance for Wilmer Valderrama's TV series *That 70s Show*.

21 October 2004: Lindsay collapses, feeling unwell while making *Herbie: Fully Loaded*. She is taken to hospital. 'My liver was swollen, I had a kidney infection and my white blood cells were accelerated. I was on an IV. They were giving me shots of morphine to numb the head pains every two hours. I was really, really white, like a ghost, and my legs were so numb from not walking, I had a walker to walk to the bathroom and back. My body didn't have enough strength to take a shower,' she told *Vanity Fair*.

12 November 2004: It is announced that Lindsay and Wilmer Valderrama have spilt up.

7 December 2004: *Speak*, Lindsay's album, is released.

11 January 2005: 'Rumors', the first single from Lindsay's album, is released.

3 February 2005: A personal injury suit is filed in Superior Court on behalf of Eddie Pamilton and Ilex Harris, who claim Lindsay's car accident the previous August left them with continuing 'pain, discomfort and physical disability. The suit seeks unspecified damages and compensation for medical expenses, lost earnings and income,' reported the Associated Press, but it was found to have no merit.

February 2005: Reports begin to appear in the press about Lindsay going to clubs and parties with friends including Paris Hilton.

Dina Lohan files divorce papers, which feature accusations that Michael had threatened her and the children.

May 2005: Photos appear in the newspapers showing Lindsay looking very thin.

She is filming a new movie, *Just My Luck*.

19 May 2005: Lindsay appears on *Saturday Night Live* and makes a joke about her weight loss, but the cast are concerned. 'They sat me down, literally before I was going to do the show, and they said, "You need to take care of yourself. We care about you too much, and we've seen too many people do this, and you're talented," and I just started bawling. I knew I had a problem and I couldn't admit it. I saw that *SNL* after I did it. My arms were disgusting – I had no arms,' Lindsay told *Vanity Fair* the following year.

28 May 2005: Michael is sentenced to up to four years in prison following guilty pleas on a variety of crimes. 'Michael

Lohan was sentenced to one and one-third to four years for a series of incidents stretching over a year, Nassau County prosecutor Joy Watson said,' Fox News reported. 'The latest occurred in February, when he was charged with drunk-driving after running his car into a utility pole on Long Island.'

June 2005: Lindsay is in a car accident days before the *MTV Movie Awards*, after a paparazzo crashes into her car.

4 June 2005: Lindsay appears at the *MTV Movie Awards* and wins the Best Female Performance Award for her role in *Mean Girls*.

19 June 2005: *Herbie: Fully Loaded* opens in the US. The film was a big hit, and Lindsay won praise for her performance. The *New York Times* said she was 'a genuine star who combines a tomboyish spunk with a sexy, head-turning strut, executed with minimal self-consciousness. Likeable but never saccharine, confident but not snooty, and endowed with the natural freckle-faced beauty of an eighteen-year-old Everywoman, Lohan seems completely at home on the screen.'

28 July 2005: Lindsay – worried about her parents' divorce proceedings back in the US – leaves the European press tour for *Herbie: Fully Loaded* and flies back to the US.

August 2005: The animated DVD *My Scene Goes Hollywood*, featuring Lindsay playing herself, is released. An accompanying My Scene Lindsay Lohan doll is in toy shops from November 2005.

4 October 2005: Lindsay is involved in an accident when her car hits a van on Robertson Boulevard in Los Angeles. She takes shelter from the paparazzi in a local antiques store. The driver of the van, Raymundo Ortega, sues Lindsay in 2007, claiming she had been drinking before she crashed. Lindsay counter-sued, and the case was settled out of court in February 2008.

5 November 2005: Lindsay releases a new single, 'Confessions Of A Broken Heart (Daughter To Father)', which comes with a video starring her sister, Ali, directed by Lindsay. She says at the time: 'It's offensive and I want it to be. I'm saying, Dad's what I needed: I was seeking your comfort and I didn't have it.'

6 December 2005: Her album, *A Little More Personal (Raw)* is released around the world.

31 December 2005: Lindsay hosts a New Year's Eve party at Prive nightclub in Miami.

2 January 2006: She is hospitalised in Miami following an asthma attack and remains there for two days before flying home to New York. 'It's the first attack since I've known her,' Lindsay's publicist Leslie Sloane Zelnik said in a statement. 'She's had attacks before, but not that many, and not recently. She's taking it easy now, she's resting comfortably.'

January 2006: Lindsay's interview with *Vanity Fair* hits the newsstands. The interview featured Lindsay talking about her relationship with her parents, her album and allowed her to talk about the various rumours that surrounded her life, from her hospital stay during the filming of *Herbie: Fully Loaded* to her relationship with Wilmer Valderrama. Controversy is caused, however, with the journalist writing that Lindsay had had 'bulimic episodes'.

11 January 2006: In response to the *Vanity Fair* feature, Lindsay releases a statement to *Teen People*, saying that her words were 'misused and misconstrued'. *Vanity Fair* responds by releasing their own statement saying that '*Vanity Fair* stands by the story'.

12 May 2006: *Just My Luck* is released to mixed reviews. *Entertainment Weekly* comments that 'even in her dullest vehicle, Lindsay Lohan exudes an unfake-able shine'.

16 May 2006: Millionaire heir Brandon Davis is taped (with Paris Hilton giggling alongside) making extremely distasteful comments about Lindsay. The clip is broadcast on the Internet, and Paris Hilton's publicist releases a statement saying: 'The only thing I want to underscore is the person making the statements was not Paris Hilton.'

26 May 2006: Brandon Davis issues his own apology. 'My behaviour on 16 May was inexcusable. What started out as a joke got completely carried away, and I am horrified at the words that came out of my mouth. I consider Lindsay a friend and I hope she accepts my sincere apology for my reprehensible actions last week.'

6 June 2006: Lindsay's publicist confirms that Lindsay has

accepted Brandon Davis's apology. 'Lindsay took the high road and accepted Brandon's apology last week.'

9 June 2006: Robert Altman's *A Prairie Home Companion*, in which Lindsay co-starred alongside Meryl Streep, is released in cinemas to great reviews. Roger Ebert of the *Chicago Sun-Times* said: 'What a lovely film this is, so gentle and whimsical, so simple and profound.'

Summer 2006: Lindsay films *Georgia Rule* in California, alongside Felicity Huffman and Jane Fonda.

2 July 2006: Lindsay begins dating millionaire heir Harry Morton and they are photographed spending the 4 July weekend in Malibu together.

26 July 2006: She is hospitalised for being 'overheated and dehydrated'. Lindsay misses a day's filming on *Georgia Rule*, causing James G. Robinson, the head of Morgan Creek Productions, to write her a letter asking her to return to work. 'We are well aware that your ongoing all-night heavy partying is the real reason for your so-called "exhaustion". We refuse to accept bogus excuses for your behaviour,' wrote Robinson.

28 July 2006: Robinson's letter appears on the website thesmokinggun.com.

August 2006: Tabloids speculate that Harry Morton is going to propose to Lindsay after he is seen at the jewellers Cartier.

3 September 2006: Harry and Lindsay are photographed on holiday in Maui together.

22 September 2006: It is reported by *People* that Lindsay Lohan and Harry Morton have split. 'Harry broke up with Lindsay yesterday at Chateau Marmont after they had dinner on the courtyard patio,' a source told the magazine.

17 November 2006: *Bobby* is released in US cinemas, with Linsday co-starring alongside Sharon Stone, Martin Sheen, Demi Moore and Emilio Estevez in a fictional account of events leading up to the shooting of presidential candidate Robert Kennedy.

20 November 2006: Robert Altman, Lindsay's director for *A Prairie Home Companion*, dies aged eighty-one. Lindsay's letter of condolence to his family is leaked to the press and she receives criticism for her bad spelling and grammar, apparently caused because it was composed on a BlackBerry, according to Lindsay's publicist Leslie Sloane Zelnik.

3 December 2006: Lindsay confirms that she is attending Alcoholics Anonymous meetings.

3 January 2007: She is diagnosed with appendicitis while filming *I Know Who Killed Me*.

5 January 2007: Lindsay has an appendectomy and goes home the following day to recover.

18 January 2007: She releases a statement to the press as it is revealed she is checking into the Wonderland Center, a rehab

facility. 'I have made a proactive decision to take care of my personal health. I appreciate your well wishes and ask that you please respect my privacy at this time.'

January 2007: *Chapter 27*, a movie about Mark David Chapman, the murderer of John Lennon, is shown at the Sundance Film Festival. Lindsay co-stars as a fan named Jude who speaks to Chapman.

1 February 2007: Lindsay pulls out of upcoming movie project *A Woman of No Importance*.

19 February 2007: Lindsay leaves the Wonderland Center after a thirty-day stay, during which time she continued to film *I Know Who Killed Me*.

24 February 2007: She is nominated for a Razzie for Worst Actress for her performance in *Just My Luck* but doesn't win. The winner is Sharon Stone for *Basic Instinct 2*.

March 2007: She appears on the cover of *GQ* in a sexy photo shoot.

March 2007: Lindsay's photos for the Spring/Summer fashion campaign for Miu Miu are released.

13 March 2007: Michael Lohan is released from prison and it is announced that he has been ordained as a minister while in jail.

20 March 2007: It is reported that ex-boyfriend Wilmer Valderrama serenades Lindsay in the Unik nightclub in New York.

May 2007: Lindsay Lohan dates Calum Best.

11 May 2007: *Georgia Rule* is released to mixed reviews. The *Los Angeles Times* said: 'It oscillates clumsily from shock to slapstick to schmaltz'.

14 May 2007: Lindsay and Calum Best are photographed at the opening of the Cove at the Atlantis Paradise Island resort in the Bahamas. They break up soon afterwards.

May 2007: Lindsay pulls out of the movie *The Edge of Love* due to 'insurance reasons', according to the fim's director, John Maybury.

26 May 2007: Lindsay is arrested after losing control of her car. It was revealed that a small amount of cocaine was found in the car.

29 May 2007: Leslie Sloane Zelnik, Lindsay's publicist, tells CBS News in a statement that Lindsay 'admitted herself to an intensive medical rehabilitation facility'. The facility in question is Promises in Malibu, where Lindsay stays for the next forty-five days. Production of her next movie, *Poor Things*, is put on hold.

15 July 2007: Lindsay leaves Promises, wearing a SCRAM bracelet around her ankle.

25 July 2007: It is announced that Lindsay has been arrested again, on suspicion of drunk-driving and possession of cocaine, following a chase in which Lindsay was pursuing the mother of her assistant.

27 July 2007: *I Know Who Killed Me* is released to scathing reviews.

July 2007: Lindsay checks herself into the Cirque Lodge rehabilitation programme in Utah.

23 August 2007: Lindsay's lawyers negotiate a plea deal on her driving cases, meaning she would not have to go to court. Lindsay pleads guilty to two counts of being under the influence of cocaine, and no contest to the charge of reckless driving. She is sentenced to two days in jail, altered to one day and ten days' community service. She is also sentenced to three years probation, and ordered to complete an eighteen-month alcohol education programme.

5 October 2007: She leaves Cirque Lodge, with her father collecting her from the facility. Lindsay dates Riley Giles whom she met in rehab.

November 2007: Riley Giles and Lindsay split. He sells his story to the *News of the World* newspaper.

15 November 2007: She turns herself into the Los Angeles County Women's Detention Center in Lynwood at 10.30 a.m., where she is searched, fingerprinted and placed in a holding cell. Then, just eighty-four minutes later, at 11.54 a.m., Lindsay is released, having completed her sentence.

November 2007: It is announced that production of *Poor Things* will continue without Lindsay in the movie.

14 December 2007: Lindsay gives an impromptu interview

to a Las Vegas radio station about her recovery, and mentions she is working on a new album.

5 February 2008: She poses for a set of photographs for *New York* magazine, based on The Last Sitting pictures taken of Marilyn Monroe six weeks before her death in 1962. 'I didn't have to put much thought into it,' Lindsay said about agreeing to do the shoot. 'I mean, Bert Stern? Doing a Marilyn shoot? When is that ever going to come up? It's really an honour.'

2 April 2008: Lindsay films a cameo role in the music video for N.E.R.D's single 'Everybody Nose'.

7 May 2008: Having started work on a new album, Lindsay releases a single, 'Bossy', which goes to number one on *Billboard*'s Hot Dance Club Play chart.

22 May 2008: The first of four episodes of *Ugly Betty*, in which Lindsay appears as Betty's old school enemy Kimmie, is broadcast.

26 May 2008: Dina Lohan's reality show about the Lohan family, *Living Lohan*, makes its debut on the E! Entertainment channel. Nine episodes are broadcast. Lindsay does not appear in the show.

June 2008: Dina becomes embroiled in a war of words with CNN reporter Anderson Cooper after he criticises the show, saying, 'I can't believe I'm wasting a minute of my life watching these horrific people.'

June 2008: Lindsay donates clothes to the Visa Swap sale, organised by charity TRAID.

9 June–18 July 2008: Lindsay films comedy *Labor Pains* with Chris Parnell, Cheryl Hines and Luke Kirby.

1 July 2008: Michael Lohan confirms rumours that he had an affair while he was separated in 1995, and there is the possibility that Ashley, thirteen-year-old daughter of his ex-mistress Kristi Kaufman, could be his daughter. He agrees to a paternity test. The matter remains unresolved.

July 2008: Lindsay launches her own fashion line of leggings, named 6126 after Marilyn Monroe's birth date.

July 2008: Newspapers start commenting on Lindsay's relationship with DJ Samantha Ronson, and guess they are a couple.

17 September 2008: The *Chicago Sun-Times* reports that Lindsay offered to host a series of events for the Democrat presidential campaign, aimed at younger voters, but her offer was declined. According to the newspaper, a source in the Barack Obama camp told them that Lindsay 'is not exactly the kind of high-profile star who would be a positive for us'.

23 September 2008: Lindsay appears to confess that she is in a relationship with Samantha during a radio interview on the show *Loveline*.

Late September, 2008: Michael Lohan sends an email to X17

Online in which he heavily criticises Samantha. Lindsay replies in a statement that her father 'is out of line and his words show how much anger he has, and it's dangerous and scary as it reminds me of how he treated my mother and I my whole childhood'. In the statement, Lindsay also confesses: 'Samantha is not evil, I care for her very much and she's a wonderful girl. She loves me, as I do her.'

November 2008: Lindsay talks more about her relationship with Samantha in an interview with *Harper's Bazaar*. In the feature, she said she wasn't a lesbian, but that she was ('maybe, yeah') bisexual.

13 November 2008: Lindsay tells *Access Hollywood* that she is slowly working on her next album, which will feature the hit 'Bossy'. As of writing, the album has not been completed.

31 December 2008: Following two weeks of reports of public rows, Lindsay and Samantha have an argument while hosting a New Year's Eve party at a club in Miami that is taped on a phone by an onlooker and posted on the Internet.

5 January 2009: Lindsay posts a message on her MySpace page saying, 'little piece of TRUE information, we did NOT break up!'

6 April 2009: She announces to the press that she and Samantha 'are taking a brief break so I can focus on myself'.

8 April 2009: It is reported that Samantha's family have visited the police to seek a restraining order against Lindsay.

April 2009: Lindsay films a spoof ad for online dating agency eHarmony in which she describes herself as 'an actress, a singer, an entrepreneur and I single-handedly kept ninety percent of all gossip websites in business'.

1 May 2009: Lindsay launches her spray tan, Sevin Nyne, to Sephora stores worldwide.

19 July 2009: *Labor Pains*, which does not get a cinema release, is shown on the cable channel ABC Family. It does not get good reviews, but it does get good ratings for the channel.

August 2009: Lindsay films a small role in Robert Rodriguez's movie *Machete* in Texas.

23 August 2009: Lindsay's Los Angeles home is burgled by The Bling Ring, who have also targeted the homes of Paris Hilton, Rachel Bilson, Orlando Bloom and Megan Fox. Approximately $130,000 worth of jewellery and clothes are taken.

September 2009: Lindsay is asked to be the artistic advisor for fashion house Ungaro.

4 October 2009: Lindsay's collaboration with designer Estrella Archs for Ungaro is unveiled at Paris Fashion Week. Reviews are mixed.

4 October 2009: Michael Lohan releases recordings of phone conversations he has had with Lindsay and her mother Dina. He explains his reasons: 'I have been trying for a year to help Lindsay with her problems privately through Lindsay, her

mom, her attorney Blair Berk and even her new attorney Shawn Holley and the courts. But when that didn't work, and the calls I was getting from Dina and Lindsay needed immediate attention, it was recommended to me to go public in order to put pressure on Lindsay.'

20 October 2009: It is announced that Lindsay is seeking a restraining order against her father.

December 2009: Lindsay travels to India to film the documentary *Lindsay Lohan's Indian Journey* for the BBC. She visits a shelter for female victims of human trafficking, and tells *US Magazine*: 'Making this documentary for BBC3 has allowed me to lend my voice to the real hardship faced by children who are trafficked. The strength of the young boys and girls I met has been truly humbling, and I hope my presence in India will bring awareness to the really important issues raised in making this film.'

12 January 2010: A devastating earthquake hits the island of Haiti. Lindsay donates profits from her 6126 clothing line to aid relief.

16 February 2010: She hosts a party in London following the Brit Awards, to raise money for aid relief in Haiti. 'I am coming to London to host a party at Altitude London,' she says in a video to her fans. 'We are doing this in aid of Haiti, and I want you to help us raise as much money as possible. All the money we raise will go directly to the Red Cross. I hope to see you there.'

10 March 2010: Lindsay appears on the *Alan Carr: Chatty Man* chat show in London.

March 2010: It is announced Lindsay will play porn star Linda Lovelace in a movie about the *Deep Throat* actress.

May 2010: Lindsay travels to the Cannes Film Festival to promote the Linda Lovelace biopic, *Inferno*. She does not return in time for a scheduled court appearance, and because she has missed some of her alcohol rehabilitation classes, is asked to appear in court on charges of violating her probation.

26 May 2010: The judge issues Lindsay with a SCRAM bracelet and strict probationary rules. Lindsay is required to submit to drug and alcohol testing in Los Angeles every week, as well as attend an alcohol education programme.

10 June 2010: *Inferno* director talks to E! News and confirms Lindsay is still cast as Linda Lovelace, despite her court appearances.

6 July 2010: Judge Revel decides at a court hearing that Lindsay has violated her probation by not attending enough classes. She sentences Lindsay to ninety days in prison followed by ninety days' rehab. Lindsay cries at the sentence. A close-up photo of Lindsay reveals she had the phrase 'Fuck U' written on one of her fingernails. Her father Michael gives interviews to the press about Lindsay's sentence.

July 2010: Lindsay does photo shoots and interviews with *Vanity Fair* and *Maxim* before starting her jail sentence.

20 July 2010: Lindsay begins her sentence at the Century Regional Detention Facility in Lynwood, Los Angeles. It is expected she will serve fewer than ninety days due to prison overcrowding.

2 August 2010: Lindsay is released after serving thirteen days. She goes directly to an in-patient rehabilitation centre at Ronald Reagan UCLA Medical Center to complete the rehab phase of her sentence.

August 2010: Lindsay's mother Dina and father Michael give separate interviews to the press about their daughter.

24 August 2010: It is reported that Lindsay has left rehab 'because the treating doctors at UCLA felt she had done everything required of her there', says her lawyer, Shawn Chapman Holley.

10 September 2010: *Machete* is released in cinemas.

20 September 2010: Lindsay fails one of her court-ordered drug tests. She posts messages to her fans on Twitter, saying: 'Regrettably, I did in fact fail my most recent drug test and if I am asked, I am prepared to appear before judge Fox next week as a result.'

24 September 2010: Lindsay is taken to jail, but released in the evening on bail. She has to appear in court a month later and wear a SCRAM bracelet in the meantime.

27 September 2010: She checks herself into the Betty Ford Clinic.

November 2010: It is announced Lindsay will no longer appear in the Linda Lovelace movie *Inferno*.

December 2010: An employee at the Betty Ford Clinic accuses Lindsay of battery. The case is dismissed for lack of evidence on 31 March 2010.

3 January 2011: Lindsay leaves the Betty Ford Clinic and moves into a rented house in Venice, California, next door to former girlfriend Samantha Ronson.

22 January 2011: She visits the Kamofie & Co jewellery store in Venice and leaves still wearing one of their necklaces. It is reported missing the following day by the staff.

9 February 2011: Lindsay is charged with theft of the necklace.

22 April 2011: Lindsay is charged with violating her probation due to the necklace theft, and is given 120 days in prison and 500 hours of community service to be spent at the Los Angeles County morgue and at a women's shelter. A pretrial hearing is set for 11 May, and the trial for the theft charge is scheduled for 3 June.

26 April 2011: Lindsay talks about her life on the *Tonight Show* with Jay Leno and receives a standing ovation.

April 2011: Lindsay is in talks to appear as Kim Gotti, daughter-in-law of mobster John Gotti, in the movie *Gotti: Three Generations* alongside Al Pacino, John Travolta and Kelly Preston.

11 May 2011: Lindsay pleads no contest in the jewellery theft case and is sentenced to 120 days' jail and 480 hours' community service. The sentence runs concurrently with her previous sentence for probation violation. It is confirmed that she is not likely to serve any jail time, but will instead be under house arrest for the sentence due to prison overcrowding. 'I am glad to be able to put this past me and move on with my life and my career. I support the judge's decision, and hold myself accountable for being in this situation,' Lindsay says in a statement.

27 May 2011: Lindsay is placed under house arrest and instructed to wear an electronic ankle bracelet. She is cautioned on 24 June for holding a party at her house and released from house arrest on 29 June.

19 October 2011: Lindsay appears in court for violating the terms of her probation, including missing court-ordered therapy sessions and community service.

7 November 2011: Lindsay serves five hours of a thirty-day jail sentence and begins more community service at the county morgue.

8 November 2011: It is announced that Lindsay will pose nude for *Playboy* magazine in their January issue.

December 2011: The January issue of *Playboy* magazine goes on sale with Lindsay on the cover.

22 December 2011: Lindsay becomes a model for Jag Jeans.

17 January 2012: Lindsay receives a glowing progress report with regards to her probation. She is also tipped to win the lead role in a movie about Elizabeth Taylor.

Lindsay Lohan
Filmography

Late Night With David Letterman (1992)

Another World (1996–1997)

The Parent Trap (1998)

Life-Size (2000)

Bette: pilot episode (2000)

Get A Clue (2002)

Freaky Friday (2003)

Confessions of a Teenage Drama Queen (2004)

Mean Girls (2004)

King of the Hill: 'Talking Shop' episode (provided voice, 2004)

That 70s Show: 'Mother's Little Helper' episode (2004)

Herbie: Fully Loaded (2005)

A Prairie Home Companion (2006)

Just My Luck (2006)

Bobby (2006)

Chapter 27 (2007)

Georgia Rule (2007)

I Know Who Killed Me (2007)

Four episodes of *Ugly Betty*: 'Ugly Berry', 'Grammy Pants', 'The Manhattan Project' and 'Jump' (2008)

Labor Pains (2009)

Machete (2010)

Underground Comedy (cameo role, 2011)

Gotti: Three Generations (rumoured, 2013)